BROKEN TURBAN

PAUL SIDHU

Hasmark PUBLISHING INTERNATIONAL

DEDICATION

This book is dedicated to my older cousin,
Billy Singh, who was my inspiration behind
writing this book.

CONTENTS

CHAPTER 1

It was a brisk mid-November day in 1977 when a tall, hulking man, six feet four inches in height and 280 pounds in weight, walked off the jumbo jet into Vancouver International Airport. He had a long, greying beard and wore a large yellow turban, a matching yellow silk Indian suit, and shoes that curled at the toes. His name was Avtar Singh. Beside him, was his young wife, Manjot, 20 years his junior. She was very pretty with her long, black, silky hair. She wore a red *saree* and sported a bindi in the middle of her forehead and a *kokka* in her nose. Gold bracelets adorned her arms, and a long 22-carat gold necklace shone on her neck. In her arms was a cute three-year-old boy named Manny, who wore a bright-red bun turban and a blue silk Indian suit in the same style as his father's.

The family had just arrived from India, and the interpreter was waiting for them. He spoke to them in Punjabi and showed them where to pick up their luggage. As they had already walked through the security screenings, he took them to the arrivals section and told them that their sponsor, Mr. Jarnal, would soon pick them up.

Jarnal had been living in Canada for about 12 years. Back home in India, Jarnal and Mr. Singh grew up together in a small village. Their fathers were cousins, but Jarnal and Mr. Singh were more like brothers. Jarnal had promised Mr. Singh that as soon as he had settled down in Canada and received Canadian citizenship, he would sponsor Mr. Singh and his family to come to Canada. Jarnal finally fulfilled his promise. Mr. Singh and Manjot felt privileged to be selected to come to this beautiful country; it was like winning a lottery ticket. Everyone else back home felt envious because they hadn't received this opportunity.

Mr. Singh, Manjot, and Manny were waiting patiently for Jarnal when suddenly, out of nowhere, they heard a voice say, "*Ohh yar*! (Hey, bro!) It's me."

Jarnal was waving and walking towards Mr. Singh through the crowd of travellers arriving with their luggage.

Mr. Singh was staring right at Jarnal but couldn't recognize him, and Jarnal thought to himself, "What's wrong with this guy?"

Jarnal kept waving, and as soon as he came up to Mr. Singh and started talking, Mr. Singh recognized the voice. He couldn't believe how Jarnal had changed after all these years. He was no longer wearing his turban and was clean-shaven. He wore Levi's jeans and a shirt covered by a sweater.

Jarnal gave Mr. Singh a big hug and said, "Hello, *yar*! It's been so long. *Kiven aa*?" (How are you?)

Mr. Singh looked at Jarnal and said, "You cut your hair and beard. Why did you do that?"

"Yes, *yar*, I've been living here for quite some time and felt like doing it. We have freedom here in this country. I liked it better this way, so I decided to do it."

Mr. Singh was quite shocked to see a clean-shaven Jarnal. He mumbled to his wife that Jarnal never should have cut his beard and stopped wearing his turban because the turban was sacred to their religion, Sikhism.

Sikhism was founded in the Punjab area of South Asia, which is now part of present-day India and Pakistan. The main religions of the area were Hinduism and Islamism. The Sikh faith began around 1500 CE when Guru Nanak began propagating a faith that was quite distinct from Hinduism and Islam. Sikhism shares many philosophical concepts with Hinduism, such as *karma, phal mukti, maya,* and *samsara.* In the days when the Mughal Empire prevailed, the Sikh community came to the defence of the Hindus, who were being forcibly converted to Islam. All gurus since Guru Nanak have worn turbans. Some reasons Sikhs wear the turban are to take care of their hair, to promote equality, and to preserve the Sikh identity. Sikh women may wear a turban if they wish. Sikhs do not cut their hair as a religious observance.

As they walked to the parking lot of the airport with all their belongings, Mr. Singh cried, "Brrr! It is so cold out here," and he took a deep breath and coughed and sneezed out the frigid air.

Jarnal responded, "Sorry, *yar,* I forgot to bring jackets for you guys. Just wait; I'll turn up the heat in the car. Remember, in India, we never had to worry about it being unbearably cold at all. When I first came to this country, I was freezing. It took me a couple of years to get used to it, and during winter, they also have snow here for at least four months."

Jarnal was driving now. He said, "We have about a five-hour drive up north. Maybe we should eat something here in the city. I know of an Indian restaurant that serves amazing dishes, tasting just like at home. I eat at this restaurant every time I come to the city. We should go too."

After eating at the restaurant, Jarnal and the Singh family continued the journey to his home.

Manjot was observing the unfamiliar but pleasant scenery—the expansive mountains and the tall, green trees, the sturdy buildings, the well-paved roads, and the many fancy cars and trucks. What she was seeing impressed her. Mr. Singh was also observing everything and couldn't believe how wonderful this country looked and how beautiful it smelled.

Mr. Singh and Jarnal came from very strict families. Being Sikh, their fathers made sure they always wore their turbans. They grew up side by side in a small, overpopulated village in northern Punjab. They had barely any electricity, irrigation facilities, or fresh water. Their families lived in concrete huts with only two rooms. All the children would share one room, and they would sleep on *manjas*—beds made of nylon webbing about two feet high and four feet long. The pollution from big industries and household *chulha* left the sky smoky and the surroundings full of dust. Food was scarce. The only foods they ate were a flour tortilla called roti and vegetables from the local fields. They would have to milk the cows every day.

While the Singh family was looking at their new world, mesmerized, Jarnal started talking again.

He said, "My friends, I have everything planned for you guys. You can stay downstairs in the basement. My wife has gotten all your beds ready, and you guys don't need to worry about it, okay?"

Jarnal continued, *"Budha pieh* (big brother), I will be taking care of you like you took care of me in India."

Mr. Singh was 10 years older than Jarnal and was close to him ever since Mr. Singh's younger brother, Ramjit, who was about the same age as Jarnal, was killed in a road accident in India when Mr. Singh was 17 years old. Ramjit was riding his bicycle on the busy highway. A bus hit him, and he passed away instantly. Mr. Singh was devastated because his father blamed him for not taking care of his younger brother and made Mr. Singh feel that it was his fault that Ramjit got killed. Mr. Singh always carried a burden of guilt because of it. Mr. Singh's father was extremely hard on him. He had to work in the wheat fields all day, take care of the family's cows, and listen to his parents' harsh comments. Mr. Singh did not receive any money from the work he did. It all went to his father, who would beat him mercilessly with a stick whenever he broke his curfew. He was never allowed to casually socialize with any of his friends and had no social interactions, except with his cousin Jarnal.

Mr. Singh asked Jarnal what he did for work in Canada.

Jarnal said excitedly, "I am the foreman at the sawmill. I've been there for eight years now. At first, I was a labourer, doing all the physical work, then I worked my way up. The foreman before me retired, so the owner of the mill asked me if I wanted to be the foreman because my attendance and work ethic were good. He was impressed that I picked up on how to do the job, and I was very detail oriented. All the other workers respected my leadership for fixing most of the problems that occurred at the sawmill. So, it was a no-brainer to make me the foreman. After you settle in for a week or so, I will get you a job there as well, my friend. That will be the plan."

Mr. Singh smiled at Jarnal, halfway to their destination, still paying attention to his face and head. Jarnal stopped at the service station for gas, snacks, and the restroom. Jarnal went in first, while Mr. Singh and Manjot stood outside, breathing in the crisp mountain air.

He looked at Manjot with a smile, saying, "We finally made it to Canada."

Manjot smiled back and said, "Yes, I am very excited. It feels like a dream. We have finally arrived here."

Feeling cold and worried about little Manny, she decided to hop back in the car, saying that she didn't need to go to the restroom. She wanted to stay with Manny while he was sound asleep.

After a few minutes, Jarnal came back outside with the snacks and drinks and handed Mr. Singh the washroom key.

"*Yar*, I'll put gas in the car. In the meantime, you can just walk right in, and to the left, you will see the washroom door. Then after using the washroom, just give the key back to the cashier, okay?"

Mr. Singh walked into the store with his chest out, long beard, bright yellow turban, and hulking frame. The cashier looked startled and felt somewhat nervous. Her anxiety rose because she had never seen a man with a turban on. She started observing Mr. Singh. He walked into the store and briefly looked at her. He was about to interact with a white person for the first time. He proceeded to the washroom. He was coughing, spitting on the floor, and using his hand to wipe snot off his nose. He closed the door, when suddenly, the cashier started knocking.

"Sir, you are in the wrong washroom."

She kept banging on the door, and when it didn't open, she went back behind the cash register and called the owner of the store. Mr. Singh walked out into the store but left the key in the washroom.

On the way out, the cashier started yelling, "Get out of here. Leave now! Don't ever come back here again."

Jarnal had finished pumping gas. He had heard the commotion and saw Mr. Singh leaving the store. Mr. Singh told Jarnal that the *gorii* was *paagal*. He told Mr. Singh to get back into the vehicle. Jarnal went back into the store and asked about what had happened. The cashier said that Mr. Singh was extremely rude. He used the women's washroom, pissed all over the toilet, put snot all over the store, and didn't even apologize. He would never be allowed there again.

Jarnal said, "I'm sorry! He is not familiar with the English language and is new to Canada."

The cashier looked at Jarnal and said, "Well, then you should have come inside with him and shown him. If he is new to Canada, it is your responsibility to guide him." Jarnal apologized again and told the cashier that she was right. She began to calm down.

A few hours after leaving the gas station, they finally arrived at Jarnal's house. On the way there, he was trying to explain to Mr. Singh that he would have to change his habits because here, in this new country, they had to be courteous and respectful—that meant no spitting, farting, removing ear wax with one's finger, or wiping snot with one's hand.

"You will learn, my friend. It will take some time. This is not India; she is probably not used to seeing a person with a turban on their head."

Jarnal continued, laughing, "Don't worry! It used to happen to me all the time in the beginning, when I first arrived in Canada. Then after a year, I stopped wearing my turban, and everyone wasn't so curious or afraid of my looks anymore, and I started fitting in. My English got better too. It will take time, my friend, it will take time."

Mr. Singh didn't look too impressed. He felt disrespect and condescension in Jarnal's comments, almost as if he were making fun of his own religion and Mr. Singh for wearing the turban. Jarnal had this arrogance, overconfidence, and cockiness that Mr. Singh had never observed when they were in India. He assumed that was because Jarnal had lived in Canada longer and was trying to show off.

They finally arrived at the town, which had a population of 3,000. At Jarnal's house, they started to unpack their suitcases.

Mr. Singh said to Manjot in Punjabi, "Jarnal is an idiot fool. He cut his hair and beard. He is trying to be like a white person. They brainwashed his mind. He is trying to act like them and be so cool. What an arrogant ass! Me and my boy will never stop wearing our turbans and will never be brainwashed by these white people. They are idiots."

At a very young age, Mr. Singh was taught to not trust Caucasian people because his grandfather had lived through the British *Raj*. From 1858 to 1947, India was ruled by the British Empire. It controlled the economy of India, which was producing more raw cotton than any other country in the world at that time. Agriculture, manufacturing, and services accelerated in colonial India. Sugarcane, coffee, tea, wheat, cotton, and jute, especially, were exported to major countries instead of merely being local cash cows. The British developed the country into an international trading partner. The British brought electric power to India and upgraded everything from irrigation to railroads to roadways. People even began to have telephones and nice cars.

Nobody had control of the country when the British first arrived. With so many regions and religions and people who knew nothing outside of their own part of the country, the British Empire took control of the land and the people of India to its advantage. Even though the Indian population was in the millions, few people were fully aware of what was happening. The British would make the Indian princes in their command rule their people, and they were paid in gold. Mr. Singh's grandfather was a slave to the British Empire and was told what to do, so Mr. Singh had certain feelings towards Caucasian people.

Manjot looked at Mr. Singh and said, "Look, Jarnal sponsored us here. He is helping us by telling us how to act and behave. He is right; we don't know anything. He has been here for 12 years, so don't be judgmental. We were living in poverty, and he has even promised you a job, so try to appreciate it. Our little boy deserves a better life in this country, and we have dreamed of moving to Canada our entire lives."

Mr. Singh went silent.

A week had passed. Mr. Singh and his family had settled into Jarnal's basement suite. Jarnal's wife, Karm, would cook and clean for them to be helpful. She tried to teach Manjot how to use the washing machine, dryer, and vacuum cleaner. Manjot had never seen these items before in her life. It was going to take a while for her to learn how to use these essential household appliances. One night, Karm took the Singh family on a tour of the city to show them the businesses, hospitals, schools, and other places in the town. Karm assured the Singhs that she would help them as much as she could. She told them not to be nervous because everyone in that small town was nice, and different types of ethnicities from around the world lived there. She mentioned that a small fraction of residents did not like people of their ethnicity, but it was best to ignore them because they were narrow-minded.

She said, "You will face such people one day, but from my experience, never let them bring you down or make you feel out of place. Remember, our children will have the best education, a better place to live, a good job, and have way more options and opportunities than we did, and eventually they will start their own families."

Manjot had been feeling a little homesick since they arrived a week before. She had started second-guessing herself and wondered if moving to Canada was a good idea in the first place because she didn't know anything about this country and felt somewhat overwhelmed by what Karm was trying to teach her. She was scared for little Manny and also felt that her husband didn't like Canada because he seemed to be upset at everything.

But Karm eased Manjot's anxiety by telling her not to be worried. She even said that Jarnal had felt the same way when he first moved to Canada.

She said, "Give yourself some time. Try to calm down and give yourself and your family a chance in this small town."

In their third week, the Singhs began to feel somewhat adjusted to the climate and the people of the town. Mr. Singh didn't like to go out in public, especially to go shopping. He felt uncomfortable, particularly while communicating with Caucasian people. The incident at the gas station had hardened this attitude, which was embedded in him from his upbringing.

Karm took Manjot shopping, and Manjot loved it. She was amazed to see the big stores and how they had every item she could think of. She felt privileged. While shopping, she couldn't help but buy novel things. She was shy at first, but her confidence grew as some Canadians said "Hi!" to her, and she overcame her hesitation and responded with a smile. After saying "Hi!" a few times, she finally overcame her shyness. She had studied English as a subject at a college in India. She felt happy that these people had accepted her and were friendly. Her husband and others implanted this image in her head about white people that wasn't so true. She felt as if she were treated better than in India and felt safer going out.

Jarnal thought it was the right time for Mr. Singh to start to work at the mill, and he knew his friend was anxious to start working as soon as possible. The mill was short of workers and some positions needed to be filled right away, especially the manual labour jobs. However, Mr. Singh first had to get his work permit papers ready, and Jarnal was trying to expedite the process. Mr. Singh still didn't understand why he couldn't work and make money immediately. He was going crazy sitting around and complaining about everyone to Manjot. Finally, Jarnal came downstairs and spoke to Mr. Singh.

He said, "Now is the time, my friend! I know you have waited and wanted to work right away, but I had to get you in at the right time. You are gonna come with me to the mill tomorrow. I am gonna to show you and get you to introduce yourself to the owner of the mill."

Mr. Singh nodded in agreement.

Mr. Singh woke up at four o'clock the next morning, got ready, and was waiting patiently for Jarnal. Jarnal didn't come down to fetch him until 6:30 a.m. They both left for the mill, and Jarnal brought Mr. Singh to Mike's office. Mike was the owner of the sawmill.

Jarnal said, "Hi, Mike! This is my friend from India. He would like to work here. His name is Avtar Singh."

Mike introduced himself and said, "Hello! How are you? Pleased to meet you."

Mr. Singh looked at him with a distressed face and quickly whispered into Jarnal's ear in Punjabi, "What the fuck is this white guy saying to me?"

Jarnal started saying to Mike, "Sorry, Mike! He doesn't understand English but is willing to work for you."

Mr. Singh interrupted, "Jass, jass, jeesss."

Mike looked at Mr. Singh and said, "I think he meant to say 'yes.' Well, I am pleased he was willing to come for an interview, and I think he will be a good fit for this job. He looks big and strong. I am going to hire him right away, and he can start tomorrow. Jarnal, can you please translate and tell Singh that he is hired?"

Mr. Singh blurted out, "Tan jou, tan jou."

Mike smiled, shook Mr. Singh's hand and said, "You're very welcome! Welcome to our team; it's our pleasure to have you."

CHAPTER 2

The next morning, Mr. Singh was again up and ready at four o'clock. It was a cold December morning, and Mr. Singh wore his bright yellow silk suit with his bright yellow turban and running shoes. A pink Barbie lunch box filled with chai tea and roti was ready to accompany Mr. Singh to the office. Manjot had arisen early to make lunch for Mr. Singh. He waited for a couple of hours before Jarnal went downstairs and knocked on the door. When Jarnal went inside, he saw Mr. Singh standing there in his white running shoes and yellow silk suit holding his little pink Barbie lunch box.

Mr. Singh said to Jarnal, "I am ready to go to work. Let's go!"

Jarnal looked at him and started laughing.

He said, "Look, my friend, before we go, we have to wear appropriate work safety attire. It is the law here in Canada. We have to be careful about our safety at work so we don't get hurt or injured. It is not like in India where anything can pass for work attire."

Jarnal had brought him a safety vest, protective eyewear, steel-toe boots, gloves, and a thick winter jacket.

Mr. Singh looked at Jarnal and said, "Why are all the Caucasian people so wimpy?"

Jarnal looked back at Mr. Singh and said, "It's not about being tough. It is simply the law. If you don't go by the rules, then you will not be allowed to work here."

Mr. Singh put on his company-provided work attire, and they arrived at the mill. Jarnal showed him how to be a block piler. He carefully watched Jarnal, who was beside him, to see if he was doing the job correctly. The prepacked bundles of wood would arrive at the end of the chain belt. Then, Mr. Singh had to stack them on a pallet on the ground. The bundles weighed anywhere between 80 and 120 pounds. One bundle would arrive every minute or so, and once the pile was eight stacks high, he would strap it down with a staple gun to secure the load. Another mill worker would take the pile away on a forklift and store it in the yard to be later hauled out on a semi-trailer. Then, he would replace it with a new pallet, and the process would start all over again. After about an hour, Jarnal was confident that Mr. Singh could do his job well, and he left for his office. He had a busy day with many calls, paperwork, and other responsibilities, being the foreman of the mill. His office was on the other side of the mill.

A few hours had passed when, out of nowhere, a siren startled Mr. Singh. He dropped the bundle of wood on the ground. It fell apart upon impact. He began to pick it up when he saw all the other employees walking away into one room and observed the chain belt slowing down and all the noise of the machinery stopping. He noticed that he was the only one left. He cleaned up what he had dropped and began to grab the wood bundles himself.

He thought, "Wow, these Caucasian people are so lazy; they stopped working. I will never be that dumb."

After about 15 minutes, he noticed everyone coming back, and everything started up again. Mr. Singh started to grab the bundles again. After another few hours, the siren sounded again, and the same things happened. Mr. Singh was puzzled that every-one was going into the room again and wondered why every machine stopped.

Many mill workers started laughing at Mr. Singh on their way out and said rude things such as, "Pink Barbie lover."

Then, one of the workers blew a whistle and waved his hand, saying, "Lunch break!"

Mr. Singh still had no clue what he was trying to say to him, and, of course, by this time, he was feeling fatigued and hungry from all the hard labour.

Out of nowhere, Jarnal came running and said, "*Yar*, I had gotten preoccupied with some other business in the office. I am so sorry. I forgot to tell you that when you hear the siren, you're supposed to stop working and have a break. The first one is 15 minutes, the second one is 30 minutes, and when you hear the third siren, it is the end of the day. You have to take your breaks. By law, you're supposed to rest and eat or drink something at lunch like roti and chai tea. When you arrive in the morning before your shift, there is a punching station that records all the hours you have worked that day. It is also located in the lunchroom. You have to punch it before you start your shift in the morning and punch it on the way out when your shift ends. That's how the office will know how many hours you have worked that day. Then after two weeks, you will receive a pay-check. Every second Friday, you will get your paycheck from the secretary's office."

Jarnal apologized again, saying that as he was extremely busy in the office with the orders, it slipped his mind that Mr. Singh was working, but he said he would try to come over to that side of the mill more often during the day to help his countryman settle into his new job.

A couple of weeks had passed. Mr. Singh was settling well into his new job, and Jarnal stopped checking up on him. In the fourth week, Mr. Singh passed the road test to get his driver's licence. Jarnal gave him his blue 1974 Chevy van that he was not driving anymore, and Mr. Singh started driving to the mill on his own. Jarnal had to start work at a different time and then drive around to neighbouring towns in the company truck doing business for the mill. Sometimes, he would come back the next day, depending on where he had gone. It made sense that Mr. Singh would commute to the mill on his own.

After a few months had passed, Mr. Singh was still block piling the wood from the chain belt onto the pallets. He was stubborn and reserved with everyone working at the mill. The only person he would communicate with was Jarnal. He would still, occasionally, work right through his coffee break and would also pick up an extra mill shift on Saturdays whenever it was available.

Mr. Singh's mindset was very clear: He had to work hard, make money, and avoid Caucasian people. He would say hello to Mike, the owner of the mill, if he ran into him, but he would never even say a word to his workmates. A Caucasian co-worker, Jack, worked with Mr. Singh on the chain belt. His specific duty was to wrap the bundle with a strap machine before Mr. Singh received it for stacking. Jack and Mr. Singh hardly ever spoke. They talked only if it had to do with the chain belt, but even then, very briefly. Jack had worked at the mill for ten years. He was a very outgoing fellow and quick with a joke. He was liked and respected by his co-workers.

One Friday afternoon, after Mr. Singh had been working for three months, the mill shift was about to end, and since it was the beginning of the long weekend, Jack and a few other co-workers decided to get some pizza and beer for everyone. Mike decided to shut down the mill early that day so everyone could meet and greet each other and have a good time.

Mike said, "Singh, come over here. Have some pizza."

Mr. Singh looked very upset because they closed the mill early. He couldn't believe that everyone was sitting around drinking beer and eating pizza. He stormed out to his car and left.

Jack said, "Boy, what's up his turban ass?"

Mark, a co-worker who started at the same time as Mr. Singh, said, "That piece of shit never says anything. Fuck that Hindu or Muslim!"

Some other co-workers agreed and laughed mockingly because he brought a Barbie lunch box to work.

By now, a couple of hours had passed, and everyone left the mill to enjoy the long weekend. Mike never heard the comments they made about Mr. Singh. He had gone to his office after briefly calling Mr. Singh over to join the rest of the employees. Jarnal was also away on a business trip that day.

CHAPTER 3

A couple of weeks later, Jack and Mark decided to play a trick on Mr. Singh during their lunch break.

Jack, Mark, and a few other co-workers were sitting in the lunchroom when Jack said to Mark, "Hey, has that turban twister ever looked funny to you or what?"

Mark said, "Yes, but that Indian smells more like fucking curry, especially when he keeps butting in the line and doesn't wait for his turn while we are about to punch our cards. That fucking diaper head should go back to where he came from."

"I agree," said Jack. "If we don't stop it, many more of his kind will come and start working at this mill."

Joe, another co-worker, was listening, and he told Jack and Mark to "cool it" and that Mr. Singh was new to this country. Joe was also Caucasian. He told the men that the way they were acting wasn't nice, and it was racist. Canada was everyone's land and everyone was to be treated equally, regardless of race, gender, or ethnicity. Everyone had a right to live and work in Canada.

As the shift started, Jack went up to Mr. Singh and said, "Hi, Singh! I need to talk to you."

Mr. Singh thought it was unusual that Jack was speaking with him face to face.

Jack said, "How are you?"

Mr. Singh looked at Jack and moved his head closer to him because he couldn't hear with all the machinery on. Mark came right behind Mr. Singh and poured ketchup on his yellow turban. Mr. Singh had been distracted by Jack and didn't notice. At the end of the shift, when it was time to go home, Mr. Singh punched his card, grabbed his lunch box, and walked to his van. On the way out, Jack, Mark, and a few other men were sitting with their lit cigarettes, laughing and pointing at Mr. Singh. He didn't understand why they were laughing at him.

As soon as Mr. Singh got home from work, Manjot noticed something red on her husband's turban. Initially, she thought it was blood, but as she came closer, she noticed it was a very smelly and sweet substance. It was definitely ketchup.

Mr. Singh was furious when he realized that someone had put ketchup on his turban. It was very disrespectful to the religion and his people because the Sikh Gurus fought to preserve their religion, and the Sikhs had risked being beheaded as a sacrifice to preserve the Khalsa faith. This disrespect towards his religion reminded him of what he had learned and seen in India. He felt inside himself the spirit of the Khalsa warrior. He was almost sure who had put ketchup on his turban.

He swore, "*Panchod!*" and threw the cup of tea across the room in a fit of anger. Manjot had to ask him to calm down.

Mr. Singh said to Manjot, "Never trust any Caucasian people. These so-called Canadian people just like to waste time smoking, drinking, and partying. They are lazy, stupid, filthy pigs. They never show up to work on time. I hate all of them."

After a few hours, Mr. Singh calmed down.

The next day at work, Mr. Singh didn't say a word because he was so upset. His expression alone could kill someone. He walked up to Jack and went for his neck with the *kirpan* on his waist. In 1699, Sikh Guru Gobind Singh gave a religious commandment in which Sikhs must wear five articles of faith at all times, the *kirpan* being one of five Ks. The Punjabi word *kirpan* has two roots: *kirpa*, meaning mercy, grace, compassion, or kindness, and *aan*, meaning honour, grace, or dignity. Sikhs are expected to embody the qualities of a *Sant Sipahi* or Saint Soldier with the courage to defend the rights of all who are wrongfully oppressed or persecuted, irrespective of their colour, caste, or creed. *Kirpans* must be made of steel or iron and are curved with a single cutting edge that may be either blunt or sharp. They can be of any size, and a baptized Sikh may carry more than one.

Jack moved at the last second as Mr. Singh swung with his *kirpan*. Jack ran into the lunchroom, and Mr. Singh ran after him. In the lunchroom, he looked around for Jack and was breathing very heavily. After no sign of Jack, Mr. Singh returned to the job after a few minutes. Jack ran to Mike's office and told him that Mr. Singh had tried to slice his throat. Mike was calm, didn't panic, and had Jarnal talk to Mr. Singh about the incident. Mr. Singh explained what led up to the fight and what Jack and his friends did to him.

Jarnal had the two men come into his office to resolve the issue. Jarnal was interpreting for Mr. Singh, and he told Mr. Singh to "never do that again." He could have been charged by the police and lost his job, or someone could have gotten seriously hurt, and he even might have had to go to jail for pulling out the *kirpan*. Jarnal apologized to Jack and Mike and told them such behaviour would never happen again. He tried to force Mr. Singh to apologize to Jack, but he never did. Mr. Singh merely walked out breathing very heavily and clenching his fists. Jarnal explained to Mike that Mr. Singh was a very religious man with old-fashioned values. He felt disrespected and deeply hurt by Jack and what he did to his turban. Mike completely understood and told Jack not to communicate with Mr. Singh. Mike had Jack work further away from Mr. Singh and had another employee work beside Mr. Singh. He told Jack to focus on the work, not on playing pranks on Mr. Singh.

Jack was shocked at what Mr. Singh had done. He hadn't expected him to react like that, neither had all the other co-workers, who had observed Mr. Singh's actions. Later that day, Mr. Singh threw down the bundled wood with authority and kept staring at Jack. Jack didn't want to start any conflicts with him. Mr. Singh was a hulking man, so there might be another fight between the both of them, and Jack and Mark were now a little afraid of him. So, they ignored Mr. Singh for a while but eventually made fun of him on occasion. Mr. Singh knew he couldn't threaten them again or his job would be in jeopardy.

A year had passed. Things never changed between Jack and Mr. Singh, but Joe, the co-worker who was working with Mr. Singh, was kind and polite to him. He would wish him good morning every day and would go over to help him stack the piled wood when the shift was over. He would also occasionally offer Mr. Singh cookies at lunch, but Mr. Singh didn't trust Joe, even though he knew he meant no harm. Mr. Singh just looked at Joe and never opened up to him or let his guard down. He kept to himself, reserved and quiet. He still couldn't trust any Caucasian man.

CHAPTER 4

M r. Singh was mostly working six days a week and decided he
had saved enough money to go to the bank for the mortgage
on a new home. Jarnal had arranged a meeting between him
and the bank manager. He had written Mr. Singh a reference letter that would get him approved for the mortgage, even though
he didn't have enough money for a down payment on the house.
However, Jarnal knew Ted, the bank manager, well, and he had
given letters to other employees, who were subsequently approved
for mortgages. At that time, houses were reasonably affordable, so
Jarnal thought that Mr. Singh would get approval for the mortgage without any problems.

Mr. Singh went into the bank wearing his bright yellow turban, yellow silk suit, and traditional curly-toed Indian shoes.

His chest was out as he walked right up to the bank teller saying, "Taad jeeee! Taaad jeeee!"

The teller said, "Sir, there is a line up over here. There are other
people in front of you, so please go and stand at the end of the
line."

A few people ahead of Mr. Singh started giving him dirty
looks, and a customer yelled, "Buddy, the start of the line is over
there. Do you understand English? Get back in the line."

Manjot came to Mr. Singh and explained to him that he had to wait in line, since she understood more English than him. She used to watch all the soap operas on television and learned fast while Mr. Singh was at work during the day.

The bank teller smiled when Manjot took Mr. Singh to the back of the line.

An older lady, who was in front of the line, came up to the bank teller since it was her turn next, and whispered to her, "What is that man wearing on his head? Look how he is dressed! He is so rude. Where did he come from? I have never seen him before."

The bank teller replied, "Ya, he does look a bit frightening. I have never seen someone wearing that on their head either, and yes, I agree he is rude. I don't know where he is from; this is the first time I have seen him. Hopefully, we won't have to deal with him at this bank."

After their transaction was complete, the bank teller said, "Have a nice day and weekend, Mrs. Rackstraw!"

Mrs. Rackstraw replied, "You too, Penny! I love your hair," and waved as she exited the bank.

While Mr. Singh and Manjot waited patiently for Ted. Mr. Singh had a finger in his ear and was wiggling it around, north to south and east to west, to remove earwax. He kept coughing and snorting, and snot was coming out of his nose.

Then he repeatedly screeched, "Quaauugaa! Quaaaga!" to take the phlegm out of his throat.

Another bank teller, Natasha, went into Ted's office to tell him that the Singhs had arrived for the meeting.

"Give me 10 minutes, please," Ted said.

"Should I offer them water or coffee, or just tell them to sit down while they wait?"

"No, let the dippers stand. Look at him, he is picking his ear and coughing so bad. He probably smells like shit. Hahaha!"

Natasha closed the door. Ted's comments about the Singh family made her uneasy.

Twenty-five minutes had gone by, and Mr. Singh was becoming anxious and impatient. Little Manny began to cry in his mother's arms because he had woken up and was hungry.

Mr. Singh walked up to Natasha again and said, "Taadd jeeee!"

As soon as he approached her the second time, Ted came out of his office and said, "Mr. Singh, come right this way. Mrs. Singh, please come."

They met for an hour, and the loan was preapproved, thanks to Jarnal's reference letter. Mr. Singh now had the mortgage for his first home. After all the paperwork was complete, Manjot was extremely happy because now they could have their own house close to an elementary school for little Manny, and they could also move out of Jarnal's basement. Mr. Singh walked out of the bank with his head held high and his chest out, like a rockstar.

Ted said to the tellers, "That Hindu is a sucker. The preapproval was for a higher interest rate, and he has to work a lot to cover it. The other wannabe white boy, Jarnal, thinks we like him and keeps giving us the clients for mortgages. He is not bad, but his accent stinks. He's starting to smell better. At least he's found Irish Spring! Hahaha!

Some of the bank tellers started laughing at Ted's racist jokes, while Natasha and a few other tellers didn't find them funny at all. They were shaking their heads because they felt he didn't have a right to speak in that derogatory manner.

Mr. Singh and Manjot told Jarnal that everything had gone well; they had been approved and were going to move into their new house near the elementary school. Mr. Singh was so happy he picked up Jarnal and swung him around like a rag doll.

Jarnal screamed, "*Yaaaaaaarrrrr.*"

He was not a tall or particularly heavy man, at five feet five inches and 160 pounds.

After Mr. Singh put Jarnal down, Manjot passed by Jarnal somewhat indifferently, and Mr. Singh said to Manjot, "Why are you acting so rude? Say thank you to Jarnal."

Manjot stared and walked away without saying anything to Jarnal.

Jarnal said, "I want you guys to succeed and live happily, so your son can have a better future." Manjot hugged Karm and thanked her, telling her how very appreciative she was for all her help.

Mr. Singh bought a two-storey house on the northeast side of the city a few blocks from Jarnal's house. It was in a new subdivision and situated in a cul-de-sac where only a few homes were already built. Best of all, it was only a few minutes' walk to the elementary school. A few days had passed, and the Singh family was settling into their new home. On the following Saturday, Mr. Singh, Manjot, and little Manny went out to buy new furniture and appliances. The company delivered everything: brand new couches, a television, a refrigerator, a stove, and even a vacuum cleaner.

Later that same day, they heard someone knocking on the door. When Mr. Singh opened the door, a clean-shaven Indian man stood there with an Indian woman.

They introduced themselves, "Hello! I'm Harry, and this is my wife, Kuljit."

Manjot recognized the young Indian lady. She would always wave to her when they pulled into their new house. She also had a young son.

They were still standing at the door when he said, "We live right down a couple of houses from you and wanted to welcome you to the neighbourhood. Did you come from the mainland, I have never seen you around?"

Mr. Singh replied, "Hello, my family came about a year ago from India. We stayed with our relative, Jarnal. He has been here for about 12 years and is the foreman at the mill where I work. Do you know Jarnal?"

Harry replied, "Yes, I do know Jarnal. I came a few years after he did, and I worked with him at the mill, but I didn't like it too much because of the physical work, and I also ended up hurting my arm. So, I decided to take a real estate course, and now I sell houses."

"Good, Good," Mr. Singh said, "I have to go somewhere."

He said goodbye to Harry and Kuljit and slammed the door when they both left. He didn't want them to know too much about his family, which is why he kept the conversation short, then ended it. In the meantime, Manjot was making tea for everyone, but Mr. Singh made sure they left before Manjot served them tea.

Manjot came back to the front door and said, "Where did they go? It was that Indian family that lives across the street. The lady looks nice; she always waves to me when I see her, especially the first few days when we were moving in. She looks like she has children, and one boy looks the same age as our little Manny. I thought by making chai tea we could get to know our neighbours and invite them inside. Did you invite them inside?"

"We don't know them," replied Mr. Singh. "It is best we just keep our distance and not get too close to them. We don't know who they are, even if they are the same colour people like us from our own country."

Mr. Singh was thinking that Harry seemed to be another "wannabe Caucasian boy with an Indian background." He came off as very flamboyant, and Mr. Singh didn't like the way he was dressed. He looked as if he were just about to go to a bar with his *Saturday Night Fever* dress pants and dress shirt on. He didn't want to associate with people like Harry.

A couple of days had passed. The men of the households were at work, and Kuljit decided to visit Manjot's house with her son, Ravy. She knocked on the door, and Manjot answered. The women liked each other right away. They had so much in common. Their sons were the same age and were happy to meet each other. Manjot and Kuljit were also from the same city in India. They talked, drank chai tea, and bonded. They felt as if they had someone to talk to in this foreign land, and they were comfortable with one another. Over the next few weeks, the women went back and forth between each other's houses, having lunch and drinking chai tea, while their husbands were at work. Little Manny and Ravy played together every day, running up and down the street and playing with G.I. Joe figures. Hide-and-seek, tag, and hopscotch were their favourite games.

Manjot's household duties were to take care of Manny, cook, clean, and do laundry while Mr. Singh was at work. Kuljit had the same responsibilities, but she also worked part-time as a housekeeper. Kuljit and Harry had been living in Canada for about eight years, so Kuljit's English was very good, and she knew where to shop around for groceries.

CHAPTER 5

One day, Manjot and Kuljit went together to the grocery store. It was the first time she had gone anywhere without Mr. Singh or Karm. The women ended up going to the shopping mall, walking through different clothing stores, checking out what was on sale, trying on all the dresses, skirts, and hats, and admiring the purses. Manjot loved it; it was a great feeling, going out, shopping, and laughing with her friend. They were having fun and didn't realize that they had been out for four hours. Manjot had forgotten about dinner. Panicked and paranoid, she hurried to try to reach home before Mr. Singh did. Kuljit's mother-in-law was babysitting the children at Kuljit's house while they were shopping, so Manjot had to pick up Manny before going home, and it was getting late. When she came home and opened the front door, there was Mr. Singh with his bright yellow turban tied tight and his steel-toe boots. His eyes were bright red with rage, and his pupils were dilated. He was sitting there motionless.

He said, "Where did you go? It's very late. Don't you know you have to stay home and make me supper? You're not supposed to go anywhere without me! You were out with that lady from next door, weren't you?"

"I went with Kuljit to the shopping mall. I had never been there before, and I wanted to see the different stores. I wanted to get clothes for Manny as well. He is going to start school soon."

Mr. Singh walked right up to Manjot, grabbed her by the hair, and said, "*Kooti*, you can't go out and waste my hard-earned money like crazy Caucasian people."

He threw Manjot to the ground. She hit the floor with extreme force to her knees. A thumping sound was heard, and something cracked. She was lying there, holding on to her knees in pain. The injury drew a little blood.

All of this happened in front of poor Manny. He quickly rushed to help his mother.

He was crying and screaming, "No, Dad, no! Please, don't!" while he gripped his mother very tightly.

Mr. Singh was just standing there, observing their reaction, staring at them with a rage in his eyes and his fists clenched. His breathing was very deep for a few seconds, and his turban was pulled back. Mr. Singh had a flashback to India of his father hitting him with a stick and the miscarriages of his first wife, Parmjit, to whom he was married when he was younger. Mr. Singh's mother blamed Parmjit for not being fertile enough to have a boy. Mr. Singh tried to have a child with her for eight years. She kept getting pregnant and kept having miscarriages. She eventually left him because of the torture she experienced. He vowed to marry a younger lady so she would be fertile and have his child.

He married Manjot, who lived in a small village right beside Mr. Singh's village. Manjot was the only daughter of her parents, and her father had passed away at a young age. Her mother was ailing and knew Mr. Singh was eager for a ticket to Canada. So, they had an arranged marriage in India. Then, a year later, Manny was born in the hospital of a larger Indian city. Mr. Singh worked as a truck driver in the city, and having been exposed to urban life, he wanted to get out of the village so that Manjot and Manny would have access to more opportunities. After a few years, Jarnal sponsored them to migrate to Canada.

Mr. Singh proceeded quietly to his room, thinking about what just happened, and fell asleep. Earlier that day at the mill, Jarnal had told Mr. Singh about the high interest rate on his new home and explained that he would be paying extra every month. He also told him that he would have to work extra to pay for house; otherwise, he would never be able to get it. Hearing about the high interest rate stressed Mr. Singh, and he was angry at Jarnal and Ted for not informing him earlier about it. Then to see his wife going out and spending money made him even angrier, like pouring gasoline on the fire, and he took his rage out on her.

The next day, there was not much conversation between Mr. Singh and Manjot. She was limping and had a swollen knee. She was hobbling to make her husband breakfast and lunch for work. Mr. Singh tried to start a conversation: "Maybe this Saturday we take Manny and buy him clothes, or maybe I can buy you something nice."

She completely ignored Mr. Singh and didn't even look at him. Mr. Singh walked out and slammed the door shut on his way to work, angered by his failed attempt to fix what had happened the night before.

Mr. Singh wasn't very fond of his new Indian neighbours, Harry and Kuljit. He despised Harry for wanting to be Canadian and acting like a Caucasian person. Mr. Singh didn't like a lot of other things about Harry, especially his car, a 1976 Trans Am with a big pair of dice hanging from the rear-view mirror. He thought that Harry was trying to show off by cruising around with the sunroof down on his sportscar, playing rock and roll music, and wearing big black aviator sunglasses on his smiling, clean-shaven face. He also wore different types of disco bell-bottom pants with his long-sleeved, colourful dress shirts. Mr. Singh showed his dislike of Harry by never waving to Harry whenever he saw him, even though Harry would always wave to Mr. Singh as soon as he saw the blue 1974 Chevy van pull into their driveway.

John was Mr. Singh's immediate neighbour in the cul-de-sac. He was an older Englishman who was about to retire after having worked as a motor vehicle mechanic for 40 years. He lived with his wife, Bertha, a retired schoolteacher. They had been living in the town for about 30 years. Their children had grown up in the town and were now married and lived in different cities in the province. John, noticing the young Indian family who moved next door, knocked on the Singh's door to try to greet them, but no one ever came to the door to answer. When John was outside mowing his lawn, he noticed Mr. Singh coming in from work. He walked over to say hi, and the hulking yellow-turbaned man came out of his van. John offered his hand and greeted Mr. Singh. Mr. Singh didn't say a word. He looked at John and merely walked right past him into his house.

John thought to himself, "Maybe he didn't understand what I said," and went back to his house to finish cutting the grass.

Later that night, Bertha asked John, "How are our new neighbours? I have seen they have a little boy as well."

John replied, "I've gone over a few times to introduce myself, but nobody ever answers the door. So, today, I thought I would go over to say hi to the father as he pulled in with his van, but he looked like he didn't understand what I was saying. He looked at me, then walked into his house. I was going to mention to him that oil was dripping from his van and that I could have looked at it for him to see why it was leaking."

Bertha replied, "They are probably shy, John. They look like a nice family, but wow, the father is a big man and looks much older than his wife. She looks very young compared to her husband. His yellow turban reminds me of reading about the *Gurkhas*. They were in the British army, helping us win the war against Hitler.

"Yes, love! I had a lot of Indian friends growing up in England and ate Indian food. I have seen so many turbans, and it is an honour to see someone wear one. Not only is it religious, but it represents a warrior and protector."

Bertha said, "John, give them some time. Let them get used to moving into this neighbourhood and let them feel comfortable. They will open up to us."

"Yes, dear!" said John.

John and Bertha Smith had an older house. It was the first one in the area before the new houses were built. They had a black Labrador named Toby.

He was very friendly, and Manny would always point to him and say, "*Doggy, doggy, ma. Ma doggy mangdaa.*" (Look! It's a dog, mom. I want a dog.)

Every time Manny went outside the house, he would walk up to his neighbour's fence and try to pet Toby. Manjot would be nervous about the dog, thinking he might bite Manny, so she would quickly grab Manny and pull him away into their backyard. At first, Bertha would peek out of the window with a smile on her face because the cute little red-turbaned kid would want to pet Toby. He seemed to like Toby, and Toby liked to be near Manny and see him almost every day.

One day, Bertha opened her sliding door on the sundeck and decided to come out into her backyard where Toby was. Manjot and Manny were in their backyard, playing.

Bertha walked up to the fence and said, "Hello, I'm Bertha. How are you?"

Manjot smiled, walked over to the fence, and said, "Hello, my name Manjot and son name Manny."

Bertha asked Manjot if Manny could come over and pet Toby because he liked him. Manjot was hesitant at first, but Mr. Singh was at work anyway, so she decided to take Manny over to pet the dog. Both women chatted for a bit. Manjot was impressed, especially by Bertha's stories that she had grown up with Punjabi Sikhs all her life. She had enjoyed the food and culture in England and was very familiar with the turban and said how beautiful it was and how the *Gurkhas* were in the British army. John also introduced himself and shook hands with Manjot and Manny. John gave Manny a lollipop. Manny was very excited as he had never received candy from a stranger. Manjot couldn't believe how nice the Smiths were, but she didn't bother telling Mr. Singh about it because he would have a fit.

One hot Saturday afternoon in the middle of summer, Mr. Singh was at home for a change, and he was putting on his new yellow turban while Manjot was feeding Manny. He heard some commotion at Harry's house, so he looked outside the window and saw a party in progress at Harry's place. Quite a few Caucasian people were standing around the front yard in swimwear, and shirtless guys were drinking beer and smoking. The barbecue was on, the music was loud, and everyone was dancing and having a good time. He even saw Kuljit in a swimsuit and couldn't believe his eyes. He was outraged and yelled for Manjot to come over and see what their neighbours were doing.

Mr. Singh said, "See, that is why I tell you to stay away, okay? He is a filthy pig, his wife is wearing no clothes, and they are giving us a bad name in the community. Just stay away from them. I don't want my son hanging out with their son anymore."

Manjot looked at Mr. Singh and never said a word. She lowered her head as she walked slowly back into the kitchen.

Manny was playing with toys in his room; it was almost as if he shut down every time his father was at home. He felt his strong presence and strict rules and always saw how he treated his mother. Mr. Singh was rude and arrogant. He felt as if he were always the smartest person, and that nobody else knew how to be a father or husband like he did. He wanted to be in control of all situations for his son and wife to have a good life. Mr. Singh wanted to keep his family safe, and that meant not having interactions with anybody.

It made Manjot feel sick and depressed. She kept her mind off her husband's behaviour by watching soap operas during the day and doing household chores. Taking care of her little boy and making sure he was always happy was her priority. Even though Mr. Singh told her not to talk to Kuljit, talking to Kuljit and Bertha made her feel good and that she could count on them as friends.

Manjot still let Manny play with Ravy, ignoring Mr. Singh's commands. The boys were the same age, and he would always want to go over to Ravy's house.

Every morning, the first thing he always said was, "Mommy, can I please play with Ravy?"

Manjot would say, "Yes, but you have to come back before your father comes back from work, okay?"

Manny would give his mother a big hug and say, "I love you."

The smile on his face was priceless to Manjot. Ravy and Manny would ride their bikes up and down the street and have water-gun fights in the yard. They would scream and jump, going from one house to the next. When they heard the ice cream truck, they would run back home to their mothers for change so they could all buy ice cream. Jaspreet, Ravy's sister, who was four years older than he was, would be the one getting the ice cream for her little brother and his friend, little Manny. They both loved popsicles.

CHAPTER 6

I t was a hot August day when Kuljit came over with Ravy and brought Manjot a bathing suit for her to try on.

She pinned it right to her chest and said, "*Saheli*, stop what you are doing and please try this on."

Manjot looked at Kuljit and said, "You are crazy. I could never wear that. My husband would kill me. He already banned me from watching any English Caucasian shows and definitely doesn't want me to be wearing anything North American. But I still watch soap operas because I love romantic shows, and my English is getting much better, but he doesn't know, and I don't want him to find out. Besides, I got so much hair everywhere on my body—on my legs, arms—so I won't look good. I will feel really embarrassed and too shy."

Kuljit looked at Manjot and said, "Look, *saheli*, I will shave everything for you, put on nail polish, do your eyebrows, cut your hair, and wax your legs and arms. You will look like the women on television. You will look and feel beautiful. We are in Canada; we have the freedom to do what we want, and our children will have the freedom as well. Please, my sister, let me at least try to do this. Don't be afraid of anyone, okay? I am your friend. We will be back before your husband comes back, but we have to hurry. Manny will be excited to see the beach and play in the sand, so let's show you and your son what Canadians do in the summertime. You have to experience it once, then judge it later to see if it is right for you or not. Me and my children always have a great time at the beach. Your husband will understand later. Please trust me."

Kuljit finally convinced Manjot to do the full makeover. Kuljit did Manjot's nails and hair, waxed her legs and arms, and put lipstick on her. It took a few hours. At the end, Manjot put on the bathing suit.

Kuljit made Manjot close her eyes, took her right to the mirror, and said, "Look, Manjot. Open your eyes."

Manjot couldn't believe it was her reflection. She looked like the women on television. She wore the biggest smile she had worn in a while. As she looked at her body in the mirror, she felt amazing, confident, and powerful. She had never felt like that before in her life.

She started crying and mumbling words as she was gasping for breath and said to Kuljit, "You are so lucky that your husband is nice and lets you live like a Canadian and have so much freedom and lets you wear anything you want. You can go anywhere, and he isn't controlling." More tears streamed down Manjot's face. "My husband doesn't even pay attention to me or Manny and tries to control me when he gets physical with me. Manny observes everything he does, and it kills me watching my son go through that.

Kuljit hugged Manjot and said, "Look, *saheli*, I am here for you and anything you need. Give him time; I think your husband still has to get used to how people live in Canada. I think he is just scared, especially after coming to a new country. Harry and I were scared to go out the first year. He thought people were living much different from us back home, but we adapted and we let ourselves into this Canadian culture. We realized we are here now, not in India. So we enjoy everything here, and the people are nice and supportive if you let them be. You can't just hide from people. That's why it's important for you and your son to get out and experience Canadian life, my friend, because our children are going to be living here for the rest of their lives and will have families here. So, let's be Canadian and respect this beautiful country."

Manjot looked at Kuljit, "My husband will never change. He hates Caucasian people and doesn't want me or Manny to hang out with you guys either, even though you are Indian. I want to feel and live like a Canadian, I do, my friend, and my son too."

Kuljit replied, "That's all right. I understand. Don't worry, he will change one day. It's all new to him, but don't you stop, my friend; you have to experience this with your son."

Manjot said, "We have been here for a year, and my husband hasn't taken our son or me anywhere fun or somewhere out as a family to spend some quality time together. It's always about work, work, work. That's all."

"*Saheli*, today we took all day to get you ready. So, tomorrow we will go first thing in the morning, okay?"

The next day, it was 38 degrees—a beautiful, hot summer day. Kuljit had convinced Manjot to go with her to the beach. She came over to Manjot's house wearing her bathing suit, and Ravy was wearing his summer swimming shorts. He had his sand pail and rubber ducky too. Manjot came downstairs and was shocked that Kuljit was standing in her front yard practically naked.

Manjot looked at Kuljit and said, "*Saheli*, aren't you shy or embarrassed?"

Kuljit said, "No, I'm not. Let's go! I got your bathing suit, and we'll put it on at the beach."

When Manjot told Manny that they were going to the beach, his face lit up, and he started running around in circles around his mother, wearing his little red bun turban.

They piled into Kuljit's vehicle and headed to the beach. As soon as they arrived, Kuljit pulled out a yellow bikini for Manjot and told her to put it on as she had done the day before. She showed her where the changing rooms were. Manjot was a little nervous and shy and thought the bikini was too revealing but saw everyone else in similar attire, so she went ahead and put it on. In the meantime, Manny and Ravy ran out to the beach with their plastic buckets and shovels, ready to play in the sand by the edge of the water. After getting dressed in the bathing suit, Manjot walked out to where Kuljit and the boys were and couldn't believe how many people were on the beach—dozens of young and old people wearing practically nothing.

Kuljit said, "*Saheli*, right here on the blanket, lie down and relax."

Manjot lay down right beside her friend. She felt the warm sand between her toes and the cool breeze from the crystal-clear water. She felt so relaxed. The boys were playing, making sand-castles, and she was having some time for herself and being with her best friend.

Then, Kuljit told Manjot to turn over and lie on her stomach. Manjot asked her why.

Kuljit responded, "I will show you why. Just do it, my friend. We have to get sun over all our bodies, not just the front side."

Kuljit started laughing, and Manjot smiled back at her. Then, out of the blue, Manjot heard a squirting sound and felt cool lotion on her back. It startled her because it was so cold on her skin.

Kuljit started rubbing the lotion all over her back, and Manjot asked, "What is that you are putting on my back?"

Kuljit replied, "It is sunscreen lotion. It protects our skin from the sun, and it helps our skin so it doesn't get damaged. I already put some on the kids while you were in there, getting changed."

Manjot started laughing, "*Saheli*, we are from India where it is much hotter than here. Why do we have to wear it here? We don't have sunscreen lotion in India and never put it on. Our skin is adapted to the sun."

"My friend, trust me. The sun has changed. The sun rays damage our skin directly because the ozone layer is weak now with all the emissions going up in the sky. I'm just trying to be cautious, okay?"

Manjot laughed, "Okay, Mrs. Canadian girl."

Kuljit giggled.

As the ladies were gossiping, all of a sudden, they heard one of the boys crying. Manny and Ravy had built a sandcastle, and another boy came over, kicked and pushed Manny to the ground, and said that it was his shovel and sandcastle. There were three Caucasian boys. They seemed a bit older than Ravy and Manny. One of the boys started calling Manny a "poo head."

"What's that on top of your head?" The boys tried to pull off his little bun and quickly ran away after an adult nearby told the boys to stop it.

Ravy was sitting there and also started to cry. They both left all of their toys behind and ran to their mothers. Manny was screaming very loudly.

Manjot held him tightly and said, "It is okay, son."

His little tears dripped down to his mother's thigh. Manjot had missed the incident, but Manny tried to explain to his mother what had happened and what the boys had done. Manjot fixed Manny's little red turban for him. She felt uneasy about what had happened and became worried. Kuljit reassured her and said the boys could play near them. She smiled and told Manjot that all children fight once in a while.

After a while, the boys wanted to go home. They had finished playing, and Kuljit lifted the boys' young spirits by getting them ice cream cones.

The boys jumped up and down, chanting, "Ice cream! Ice cream! Yay! Yay!"

The ice cream stand was at the end of the beach where their cars were parked. At the ice cream stand, Harry pulled in with his Trans Am, which had a loud, roaring engine. His cousin, Vik, was a passenger. They both hopped out.

He gave Kuljit a big hug and kiss and said, "Honey, let's stay for another hour. My cousin is up to visit from the mainland. He wanted to check out the beach. We also brought some Kentucky Fried Chicken for everyone to eat. We will have a small picnic and go home, okay?"

The men pulled out a cooler with cold pop to give to the ladies and the boys, and they had some cold beer for themselves.

Manjot said, "One more hour only. I have to get home on time."

Kuljit replied, "No problem, my sister. Let's go lie down for an hour and enjoy the sun for a bit longer."

Manny was eating very quickly. He had never had this kind of food before. He was stuffing the fries in his mouth and drinking the Coca-Cola.

He said to his mother, "I love fried chicken . . . mmm . . . I love fried chicken, momma!"

Manjot had a piece of chicken and some fries.

She said to Kuljit, "Wow! This is so yummy. Where did you get this?"

Kuljit replied, "At a restaurant called Kentucky Fried Chicken."

Manjot and Manny, of course, had never tried it before. Everything was a brand new experience for them.

Manjot told Manny to thank Uncle Harry for the food.

Manny went up to Harry with his hands together and said, "Thank you, Uncle."

Harry was not his uncle, but Manny called him Uncle Harry anyway, out of respect for his elders, and it is a common way of addressing people in India.

Harry replied, "You are most welcome. Enjoy, *beta*!"

Earlier in the day, Harry and Vik had gone to the local bar to play pool and drink some beers. Vik had had a few too many beers and was a little drunk. He noticed someone sitting beside Kuljit that he had never seen before, so he decided to walk up to where they were and sat right beside Manjot. He introduced himself, telling her that he was from the mainland and that he usually came up for a couple of weeks to visit his cousin Harry in the summer and that he had been in Canada for about 10 years. Manjot also introduced herself, and they both started engaging in a simple conversation. Harry had gone to park his car in a proper parking space, and Kuljit took the boys to the washroom. Vik started complimenting Manjot. He was around the same age as she was and, obviously, much younger than Mr. Singh. He spoke politely to her and was sincere in the way he asked her if she needed anything at all, but, mostly, he was making her laugh. He was telling her jokes, and she tried to keep her laughter inside until her stomach hurt.

Vik was strong with broad shoulders and had hair and sideburns like Elvis. He had a beautiful smile on his clean-shaven face. Manjot felt a slight attraction to him. Vik, with alcohol on his breath, complimented her legs by grabbing an ice cube with his two fingers, and starting from the bottom of her legs, he grazed her legs all the way up to her thigh where her bikini started and said it would cool her off. Manjot was startled. She immediately got up, wrapped a towel around her waist, and ran towards the bathrooms where the boys and Kuljit were. She couldn't believe what was happening to her.

She said to Kuljit, "We have to leave now."

At the same time, she looked back at Vik, and from a distance, he was waving to her and said goodbye with a smile. She paused for a minute to take it in. She felt a little embarrassed about the whole situation but didn't tell Kuljit.

As Kuljit was driving home from the beach, Manjot was telling her to hurry up and get home before her husband got home. She didn't want him to be angry at them because they ended up staying an extra two hours at the beach.

Kuljit said, "Look, the kids had fun, so much fun at the beach. They played, ate ice cream, ate fried chicken. We had a good time relaxing. Did you have a good time, my *saheli*? I know it was your first time at a beach."

Manjot said, "Yes, I did, my sister. I had an amazing time."

In the meantime, she was thinking of Vik—his big brown eyes, his beautiful smiling face talking to her, and how he touched her legs. She couldn't believe how she felt—as if she were dreaming. She felt very alive and liked the attention she was receiving from Vik since she wasn't getting any from her much older rude husband.

Manjot asked Kuljit, "Does Vik come very often to your place?"

Kuljit replied, "He does for a week or so every summer. Why are you asking? How do you like Vik? You guys seemed like you were in a long conversation with each other."

"Well, he's good looking like a Bollywood movie star and seems like a nice guy."

Kuljit started laughing and said, "Yes, he indeed is. I think my husband has been trying to copy him ever since he came to visit us a few years back. He comes up every summer since he is from the mainland. There is a bigger population of our people there. Nobody dresses like him around here, and Harry tries to copy him. Sister, you know what? He is single."

Manjot started laughing, "Stop it, stop it. I can't do that; I'm married."

Kuljit finally arrived at Manjot's house.

Manjot pointed to a car and said, "*Saheli*, that red car was at the beach all the time while we were there. I know it was the same car that drove by slowly just now in front of the house. I have seen that car before. I just can't remember whose car it is. I'm scared, Kuljit."

Kuljit said, "Don't worry about it. Your mind is playing tricks on you because you're too nervous. Call me tomorrow, okay?"

"Okay," said Manjot, "Anyway, I'm getting late."

Little Manny was tired from all the playing and running around. Manjot grabbed him with one arm, threw him on her shoulders, and brought him inside the house. She put him in the bathtub and turned on the warm water. She started thinking about Vik again, how he was so nice and polite to her and made her feel special when he touched her leg. She then immediately snapped out of her dream and went into the kitchen to make Mr. Singh some dinner. She heated some leftover *subjee* and made roti for him, knowing he must be coming home soon. Then, all of a sudden, the door opened and slammed shut. Manjot placed Mr. Singh's dinner on the table as soon as he came in through the front door. Then she slowly sneaked into the bathroom where Manny was in the tub.

She turned off the tap and began scrubbing little Manny's back when Manny asked his mother, "Mommy, can we go to the beach tomorrow again? Please, mommy."

Manjot replied sharply, "Shhh, *puth*! Keep quiet! Your dad is home, okay. Don't talk about it now."

Manny said, "Okay, mommy!"

Manjot said, "After your bath, you need to go to bed. Okay, my beautiful son?"

Manny agreed. Then Manjot tucked him in, kissed him, and told him that she loved him. At that moment, she realized that she was going to try to give Manny as much experience and freedom as he needed to explore the world and that she would support her little boy in anything he desired and whatever his goals were. She would not let him be deprived of his childhood joys because of Mr. Singh's rules, even if it meant disagreeing with her husband. Even if he didn't realize what she was doing, it was a big step for Manjot to bravely stand up to Mr. Singh. She knew it was going to be tough because of Mr. Singh's strictness and tough love. She was ready to face the consequences. She'd had enough, now; it was the time to stand up to him, but she knew that was not a traditional Indian way for a wife to be. With his narrow-minded way, Mr. Singh would never give anybody a chance to have liberty, even if they were of the same race. He was stubborn and felt he was always right.

Manjot walked back into the kitchen to see her husband.

Mr. Singh asked, "Why is this the same dinner as the other day? It's the same *aloo gobi* that you cooked yesterday."

He noticed Manjot looked a bit different and asked her where she went that day.

She replied, "Nowhere!" because, of course, she didn't want him to know she had gone to the beach.

Manjot handed him his towel so he could take a shower. He took it, mumbling something in a disgruntled manner, and as he was about to go into the shower, he observed that Manjot's face was looking brighter but ignored it because he was tired.

Manjot returned to her room shortly after that. She went to bed. Her room was beside Manny's, just in case he woke up from his nightmares, screaming and too scared to go back to sleep. He had started having bad dreams last year, and Mr. Singh couldn't tolerate it. He didn't want to be disturbed at night by the slightest noise because he had to go to work the next day. So, he started sleeping in a bedroom further down from Manny and Manjot's room. They both agreed to Manjot sleeping in the bedroom right beside Manny so he felt safe.

Since it was getting late into the night, Manjot closed her eyes and fell asleep. She dreamed about the beach, where it was just her and Vik. He was touching her legs and kissing her. Manjot was aroused in her sleep and started moaning. She woke up hot and sweaty. She was breathing heavily. She realized it was a dream and not real, but she felt as if she had made love, and the feeling was real. She slowed her breathing and calmed down.

She then lay back on the bed, thinking about her dream for a minute. "Do I really have a crush on Vik? Am I secretly liking him and not admitting my feelings, or is it just a dream?"

On the other hand, she knew in her heart that she could never leave her husband, and maybe she felt lonely since it had been about five years since she and Mr. Singh had had sex. After Manny was born, all physical and emotional contact with each other disappeared. They didn't even exchange a hug or a kiss, and Mr. Singh showed no positive emotion towards his son either. When Mr. Singh became angry, he physically hurt them. He never spent any time with Manny or even played with him. He never asked how he was or took him and Manjot anywhere. He even forgot their anniversary and Manny's birthday. He was a stubborn and strict brute who wanted his wife to simply cook, clean, and take care of Manny and make sure he went to school, while he worked, because that's what was expected of wives when Mr. Singh grew up in India.

His father was very strict and had reminded Mr. Singh every day that it was his fault his little brother Ramjit was killed in the accident. Mr. Singh's father never showed any emotion towards him, so Mr. Singh continued this behaviour in his marriage and towards his son. That's the way he wanted to live—without any outside interference or interaction, especially with Caucasian Canadians. Mr. Singh was a selfish, intolerant, and inflexible man who didn't care about anybody's feelings. He was like a military tyrant.

The next day, Kuljit and Ravy visited Manjot. The two women drank chai tea while the boys were playing downstairs with toy army men. The ladies discussed how much fun they had at the beach and the great experience they had. They talked about how beautiful the beach was and how it felt to be a Canadian and have all the freedom to lie there without a care. They spoke about the surroundings, the mountains, sand, beautiful water, all the people enjoying themselves, and how the kids loved it, especially Manny. That was his first beach experience. The only disappointing thing had been when those kids had pushed and kicked him and tried to pull off his little red bun. They were not used to seeing turbans, and Manjot thought people were going to pick on Manny in the future as well.

Kuljit said to Manjot, "Have you ever thought of giving Manny a short haircut like Ravy's, so he can fit in? I know our religion prefers to keep hair long, but you have a choice. You can still keep our religion with or without it."

Manjot looked at Kuljit and said, "Yes, I have thought about it. I would like to cut his hair, but at the same time, my husband is too strict. He would never allow that, but as Manny gets older, he can make his own decisions, and I will stand by him. I think being in Canada and living with all sorts of different religions, he will have the freedom up here to make his own decisions as he grows older."

Then Kuljit said, "I almost forgot. Speaking of haircuts, I have to give Ravy his, before school starts."

She told Manjot to register Manny at the school quickly because, in about two weeks, classes were going to start, and this was going to be the first year of school for Manny and Ravy. Luckily, they were the same age and were most likely going to be in the same kindergarten class. Kuljit said that Jass was going to be in grade 3 and that she had been through the back-to-school drill. She assured Manjot that her daughter would "keep an eye out for Ravy and his buddy."

Manjot said, "Thank you! I will go tomorrow and register him. Can you please come with me?"

"Of course, *saheli*! Let's go tomorrow, and we will go shopping for school supplies as well."

Later that day, close to supper time, Mr. Singh came home at the same time Kuljit and Ravy had returned home. Manjot had dinner prepared for him, and he sat down and began eating as he usually did. Manjot would usually go to her room when he was about to eat, but this time, she stayed in the kitchen. Mr. Singh was looking at her, keenly anticipating what she was about to say.

She said, "I have to register Manny at the school tomorrow so he can start kindergarten class in a couple of weeks and have to get him some clothes and school supplies."

He was staring at her with his yellow turban on and his eyes bloodshot, not saying a word for some time.

Then he muttered, "School, school!"

He looked surprised, but at the same time, he felt relieved. He ate his dinner and went to bed.

The next day, when Manjot went into the kitchen to make Mr. Singh his breakfast and lunch for work, there was some money left for her on the counter so she could register Manny for kindergarten. She felt happy that for once, Mr. Singh didn't make it impossible for her to do something. She was so excited, she called Kuljit and told her all about it.

Even Kuljit was surprised and said, "Maybe he's changing."

Mr. Singh still didn't like that Manjot spent time with Kuljit, but at the same time, he knew that she was helping his family. So, he kept quiet, and as his goal was to get Manny an education, he was slightly less disagreeable when it came to doing things related to school. He wanted the best for his son so that he could grow up to become a lawyer or a doctor.

The women registered the boys. They would receive the school schedule in the mail in about a week. Then they went shopping.

Manjot told Kuljit, "My husband wants to go out this Saturday to buy me a new dishwasher for the house."

"Oh, really? That's nice. It will save you from washing dishes by hand all day."

It was Saturday, and Mr. Singh took a day off to buy his wife a dishwasher. They arrived at the appliance store. Mr. Singh walked with his hands crossed under his armspits with little Manny and Manjot right behind him.

Mr. Singh walked right up to the cashier and said started calling, "Hello! Hello!"

The cashier pleasantly said, "Sir, a sales associate will be with you in a minute."

After a few minutes, a young sales associate said, "What are you looking for today, sir?"

Mr. Singh said, "Wash wash," and then he started to move his arms as if he were washing dishes. The sales associate was confused. "Are you looking for a washer and dryer?"

Mr. Singh shouted, "Nooo! Nooo!" shaking his head and again pretending to wash dishes.

The sales associate said, "Maybe my manager can help," and left Mr. Singh at the front of the store to get his manager, Len, to come and help him.

He said, "Len, there's a man in the front of the store. I don't know exactly what he is looking for, but can you please help him?"

Len said, "No problem, I will help the customer," and as he walked out, he noticed a tall Indian man wearing a yellow turban with his young family. At this point, his instinct was to not talk to him, but he did anyway.

Len said rudely, "What are you looking for? I'm busy."

Manjot said, "Dishwasher."

Len said, "Why didn't you say that before?"

Mr. Singh said, "Sorry, sorry!"

Len took them to the dishwasher section and said, "There you go! The prices are on them."

Mr. Singh looked at Manjot and then at all the prices and said to her, "*Mahenga hai.*"

Len left them and went back to his office while they were deciding.

Then he realized Mr. Singh was following right behind him, saying, "Too expensive, man," and offering a lower price.

Len looked at him and said icily, "Take it or leave it, buddy."

Mr. Singh stormed out of the appliance store and shouted at Manjot, "Hurry up! Let's get out of here."

He looked at her and said, "*Panchod gora*! They have their prices way too high for me."

Manjot looked at Mr. Singh, saw his frustration, and felt a little ashamed about how they were treated and how Mr. Singh was too cheap to buy the dishwasher.

Meanwhile, back at the appliance store, Len walked up to the sales associate and said, "Don't ever come to get me when you see those fucking Hindus, all right? I fucking hate those brown Pakis. See how the dumb freak was standing. He knew no English. He was wearing his pyjamas and looked like Bigfoot with a fucking turban on. He smelled like cow shit, and the fucker followed me right to my office."

The sales associate was very surprised at how Len was reacting but agreed to obey him since he was his boss.

Len went on, "You know, his wife looked pretty hot. Hahahaha! I would take her out."

The sales associate didn't say anything but was disturbed by how Len was behaving.

CHAPTER 7

It was the start of another work week for Mr. Singh, and Manjot's day was routine until she noticed the red Chrysler again, going slowly by her house. She tried to see who was driving it, but it drove away. She ignored it, even though it gave her the chills. She just closed the blinds and continued cooking, cleaning, and chatting with her friend on the phone.

As for Manny, he was with Toby. He loved the dog very much. The first thing he would do when he woke up would be to run over to the fence where the Smiths lived and pet Toby. He would bring some food for Toby as well. Bertha would smile at Manny and encourage him to play with Toby. She felt a special place in her heart for Manny. She saw how he loved Toby and felt he was bonding with him. Bertha baked a lot, and sometimes she would offer Manny and Manjot freshly baked cookies hot out of the oven, and they would eat them appreciatively. Sometimes, when John was not busy, he would come outside to play with Manny and Ravy, and he even gave Manny a kite to fly. Manny liked John because he would pay attention to him and teach him a variety of interesting things, such as how to build a paper airplane. He even taught him how to build a model airplane from a kit. The Smiths were kind to the Singhs, and Manjot would let Manny go over to their house whenever he wanted to. She had no problem with that because her son felt very comfortable at their house.

One day, Mr. Singh's van died just before he arrived home from work, and John saw his neighbour trying to push his van by himself.

He came over and tried to help Mr. Singh, but Mr. Singh shouted, "Nooooo! Nooooo!"

John, being a retired mechanic, popped open the hood and saw a wire was loose. He fixed it and told Mr. Singh to hop in and give it a start. Mr. Singh hopped in, turned the key, and the car started. John shut the hood and gave Mr. Singh the thumbs-up sign. Mr. Singh said nothing—not even a simple thank you— and drove home. Later that night at dinner, Mr. Singh was bragging to Manjot about how he got John to help him when his van died.

He said, "*Saala kamla gora.* He came over to help. I said 'No, go home!' to the old man. I didn't think he could do anything, and I could have started it myself."

Manjot just looked at him and felt sorry for John, saddened by how Mr. Singh had treated him. She knew John was trying to help him because he was a good and caring old man.

The next day at work, Jarnal told Mr. Singh that he wanted to talk to him in his office. Jarnal told him that a few weeks ago his wife had been in a bathing suit while out with Harry and Kuljit. They were at the beach, and there had been another man there. Jarnal said that he heard this through friends of Harry, and they were specifically talking about Mr. Singh's wife and son, who was wearing a turban. She was lying there practically naked, laughing and enjoying the company of another man.

Mr. Singh was shocked and became very angry. He left work in the afternoon, went to the liquor store, and grabbed some rye whisky and coke. He drank the whole bottle in the Chevy van and drove around trying to pick up some prostitutes on the street. He gave one of them some money, and in the middle of their liaison, he started biting her. Feeling threatened, she took his money, jumped outside the Chevy van, and ran away. It was around ten o'clock, and Mr. Singh was on his way back home. Manjot became worried, wondering where Mr. Singh was. She didn't want to call Jarnal to see where he was; that would be her last option.

Mr. Singh pulled up at his home, weaving into the driveway. The headlights were still on. As he opened his van door, he stumbled onto the ground. He got up with the empty 40-ounce bottle in his hand. He was swearing very loudly, calling Manjot a *paan chotti*. He threw the bottle against the front door, and the neighbours heard all the yelling and screaming and wondered what the matter was.

John immediately went outside to see what was going on. Then he went over to the Singh's house. The front door was open, and Manjot was lying there, knocked out on the floor. Manny was on the ground, crying and holding on to his mother. There was a bump on his head. Mr. Singh was so intoxicated that he had been kicking Manny on the ground. He stumbled and fell over onto the couch. He got up to try to take a swing at John but missed and fell onto the kitchen floor. He just lay there passed out. John eventually helped Manjot get up. He noticed a little blood coming out of her mouth and a big black shiner on her eye and told her to sit down on a chair. He got some ice and applied it to her eye. Bertha came in, picked Manny up, and held him in her arms, hugging him while he was crying. She asked him if anything hurt and saw a bump above his eye. The Smiths were wondering if they should call the police and asked Manjot and Manny to spend the night at their place, but Manjot asked them to leave.

"Please just go. We will be all right. And don't call the police. Just go."

The Smiths looked at each other and decided it wasn't their business to get involved but assured Manjot if she needed anything to never hesitate to come over or call for help.

The next day, Manjot got up and made Mr. Singh his breakfast and his lunch for work with a black eye and swollen lip. She pretended the incident hadn't happened, and away he went to work. Something inside Manjot felt as if it died after the incident with Mr. Singh. She knew she was his wife, and that was that! She had to obey Mr. Singh. They expressed no feelings; it was merely a paper marriage, and they were stuck forever. She realized she could never leave. She would pray to help her cope with her situation and emotions, thinking of India.

She thought to herself, "What if I had never married this man?"

She would have been better off, but then Manny would have never been born. And she was so thankful to have him. Her love for her little boy was undeniable.

Then she started to think she should leave with her boy for good. She felt increasingly confident that she could do it. Her fear started to become anger towards Mr. Singh. She decided the situation was not right; something needed to change, and soon.

John and Bertha became consciously observant of Mr. Singh. They would see him leave for work in his van, and then the Singh's house would be as silent as if someone had gone on vacation and left their home empty—no Manny coming over to pet Toby, no Manjot outside using the clothesline, no Ravy or Kuljit coming over. It was like a ghost house. The Smiths were a little worried.

CHAPTER 8

A few days had passed, and all the Smiths saw was Mr. Singh come and go from work with no sign of Manny or Manjot. Then, one day, Kuljit knocked frantically at their door. She asked Bertha if she had seen or heard of Manjot because she had been calling her, and there had been no answer. Bertha said she hadn't seen Manjot and didn't tell Kuljit what had happened that night at the Singh's house. The next Saturday morning, Manny went outside but never came to pet Toby. He just played by himself with his toys, but he was looking at Toby as if he wanted to pet him. Manjot went outside to sit and watch Manny play, and Mr. Singh went outside wearing his bright yellow turban and his silk suit. He tried to sit beside Manjot as he was drinking his tea. Manjot got up and moved her chair away from him. Manjot's expression was a clear message to Mr. Singh. She didn't even look at him. Bertha was watching them through her window, worrying about Manjot and Manny.

Bertha said to John, "Well, since that night, there hasn't been any more fighting. It has been very quiet at the Singh's house, and it looks like she is not happy with Mr. Singh."

John said, "Yes, it definitely looks like Manjot doesn't want to be around her husband. She looks extremely unhappy. I hope

Singh doesn't act like that again. We will have to call the police if there's a next time like this. Dear, nobody deserves to be treated like that."

Bertha said, "You're right, John. I don't want to see that little boy or his mother hurt."

Manjot was still angry at Mr. Singh. She knew why he did what he did, but she didn't feel as if she had done anything wrong just because she went to the beach with her son and friend.

Manjot decided to tell Kuljit everything that had happened that night. She invited her over and explained she had a black eye that she didn't want Kuljit to see, and how Manny was also hurt by Mr. Singh's kicks. She told Kuljit that it was all because she went to the that day. Kuljit hugged her friend and couldn't believe what Mr. Singh did. She immediately told Manjot to pack her and Manny's bags and come over to her house, but Manjot was nervous about leaving.

She said, "I don't know, *Saheli*. I really don't know if I should take this step. I might make things worse in our relationship by doing so."

Kuljit said, "If you don't, he will keep doing this. Show him this is not right. We are here in this new country; you can't keep things as they are. Your little boy could have been seriously hurt, same with you. Let me tell you about a situation like yours. There was a lady who was getting beaten by her husband. One day, her husband beat her so bad that she died in the hospital because of the injuries caused."

Undecided, Manjot took her friend's advice and followed her own gut instinct. She packed her and Manny's belongings in a suitcase and left. She told Manny that they were going to Kuljit's house for a few days. Manny was so excited that he could be with his friend around the clock.

The Smiths were looking out their window and saw Manjot loading her suitcase and other belongings in her friend's car. They assumed she was going somewhere safe.

Bertha said, "Look, John. They are leaving with Manjot's friend. Maybe she is moving out." Being curious, they observed the Singh's house all the time, wondering what was going on.

Mr. Singh came home from work. He pulled into the driveway with his van, walked into the house, and slammed the door as was his everyday ritual. He noticed his wife and son were not around, and no dinner was made. He went to the bathroom, took a shower, got dressed, and went back into the kitchen. Still, he saw no sign of Manjot or Manny. He became upset with his wife for not making him dinner. He suspected she was busy spending time with Kuljit, so he got into his van and drove to Kuljit's house. He knocked on the door hard, calling for Manjot. Kuljit knew it was Mr. Singh but told her husband not to answer the door. Mr. Singh became angrier. He called Jarnal to see if his wife went to his house with Manny. Jarnal said that he hadn't seen Manjot or Manny and maybe she was with the guy she met at the beach. Mr. Singh was fuming and drove around aimlessly the whole night, looking for his family, eventually returning home at dawn.

He went straight to work, very angry about his family. He made numerous calls to his house and Kuljit's house from work. Finally, Manjot answered the phone at Kuljit's house.

Enraged, Mr. Singh asked her what the hell she was doing. "You are embarrassing me and yourself. I am calling around to strangers' houses looking for you, *panchod*! You are a fucking disgrace. Are you with the other guy, you slut? Don't ever come back, slut!"

Manjot started crying. Manny saw his mother in tears. He quickly came over, held her hand, and said, "Mama I love you."

Holding her son's hand, she slowly put down the receiver and held on to her son with tears rolling down her cheeks, remembering her father holding his only daughter, loving her, and playing with her when she was a young girl. He treated her like his little princess who was worth gold to him. He never swore at or hurt his daughter and loved her more than anything in the world. He promised that one day, she would have a great husband who would take care of her, love her as he did, and treat her honourably and with respect. That was the only wish he had for his child and, of course, health and happiness for her life. Unfortunately, he died when Manjot was about 14 years old.

Kuljit was feeling bad for her friend and told her to not answer the phone again. "My sister, leave him alone. You deserve better than that."

Mr. Singh was shocked and infuriated at Manjot's actions and started blaming Manjot for staying at Kuljit's house. He called Kuljit's house repeatedly after work and in the morning before work and would drive by hoping to talk to Manjot or maybe just to see her. It had been a week since Manjot talked to Mr. Singh. She was trying to stay strong and hold her own. She was hurt by Mr. Singh both physically and emotionally.

Manny was too young to understand what was going on; he was just loving the idea of staying at Kuljit's house, playing with Ravy day in and day out. After a while, Manny started wondering why they weren't going back home and said to Manjot that he didn't miss Papa. This admission made her feel guilty.

She told Manny, "We will go soon, okay son. Go play with Ravy."

Kuljit told her that she was doing the right thing and that it took courage to do what she did. She said many women put up with abuse, and they didn't have the guts to stand up for themselves and show their husbands that they couldn't be messed around with like that.

After two weeks, Karm called Kuljit's house to talk to Manjot. Kuljit was hesitant to give Manjot the phone at first but decided to see if Manjot wanted to talk to Karm. Manjot was somewhat concerned about Mr. Singh since she hadn't talked to him in a while and wanted to hear what Karm had to say. She had great respect for Karm because she had shown and taught her new things when she first came to Canada. Karm explained that Mr. Singh had been staying at their place for the last couple of weeks. He was devastated and wanted them back. He had been crying in front of Karm and Jarnal saying he truly missed his wife and little boy and that he would never interfere with Manjot again. Manjot was indecisive at first with good reason, but because her heart was forgiving, and she trusted her judgement, she decided to go back home. A few days later, she told Kuljit that she was happy to have a friend like her and that maybe her husband had learned his lesson and changed, and Manny could be back with his father.

Kuljit said, "Well, you know where to come if he acts up again. Tell him what you want before you go back home, and make sure you tell him you will call the police next time."

Manjot packed up her and Manny's clothes and called Mr. Singh. She told him that if he ever touched her boy or her again, that would be the last time they were ever going to stay with him, and she would call the police. Mr. Singh didn't say a word. He was experiencing culture shock. It seemed as if his wife had a voice. She was standing up for herself and not fearful. Mr. Singh had to digest his many mixed emotions, which was an unusual experience for him. He wanted to talk to Manny and for them to come back home as soon as possible.

The Smiths saw Manny and Manjot finally return with their suitcases after a few weeks when Kuljit dropped them off.

Mr. Singh dearly missed his wife and son, and when he came back from work, he gave them both a big hug. It was the first hug he had given his wife in five years, and it was the first time that little Manny had received a great big hug from his father. Manny didn't want to let go. He gripped onto his father so hard. Tears shone in Mr. Singh's eyes. Manjot observed how Manny was hugging his father so tightly. She felt happy, and tears of joy and relief rolled down her face to see her husband caring for her little boy. Mr. Singh told Manjot and Manny that he missed them and loved them so much. He wanted his son to do well in the new school year, so he decided not to be such a controlling bully and to support Manjot from now on.

Manjot was slowly taking on a renewed role in the house. The tide shifted towards her and her little boy, and Mr. Singh was left to be the observer, not the aggressor. From the moment Manjot was back home, she showed Mr. Singh that she was in control. He mellowed after the experience, and their homelife became calmer. Manjot's leaving made him realize what was important. It also seemed as if Mr. Singh's age was starting to soften his aggressive attitude.

September was the beginning of a new school year, and all the children had their brand new clothes, backpacks, lunch boxes, and school supplies ready. It was the first year of school for Manny and Ravy. They were enrolled in kindergarten.

CHAPTER 9

As Manjot walked Manny to his class, Kuljit, Ravy, and Jass also followed. Manny was very shy. He had never seen so many children his age. He held on to his mother's hand very tightly and didn't want to let go.

Then the teacher came over with a big smile and said, "Hello, young man. I am your kindergarten teacher. My name is Mrs. Lesner, and what is your name?"

Manny smiled and didn't say anything at first. Then Manjot encouraged Manny to say his name. It took him a few minutes, then he said, "Manny."

The teacher said, "Hi, Manny! that is a beautiful name for a nice boy. Come! Follow me, please. I will show you where to put your jacket and your lunch box. If you ever forget where to put your stuff, your name is written on here, see?"

"MANNY" was written in big, black letters on yellow masking tape. Mrs. Lesner would show all the pupils in her class where their cloakroom was, and it was Ravy's turn next.

The first day of school was short, and Manjot was impressed with how nice the schoolteachers were and how everyone treated her Manny. She thanked Kuljit for being there for her and explaining everything, helping her to register her boy for kindergarten.

Kuljit responded, "Don't worry, *saheli*. I will make sure our kids are safe. Jass will look out for them. Since she is older than them, she can walk them to school."

Manjot smiled and thanked her. Kuljit told her that Jass had Mrs. Lesner when she was in kindergarten. She was a very pleasant teacher, so she already knew that their children would be fine. Jass told Manjot that Mrs. Lesner used to bake her cookies and make scrambled eggs for all the kids, and it was so much fun.

Manjot looked at Jass and said, "*Puth*, that is so nice. Thanks for telling me that."

For the first few weeks, Manjot would walk Manny to school because he was very shy, but after five weeks, he started walking with Jass and Ravy. It took him a while to get used to it, but he had to because Manjot had to start working as well, picking up shifts for housecleaning for Kuljit. She was always asking her friend for some part-time work, even to get out and do something when Manny was at school, so Kuljit got her a job.

Manny got up early every morning, brushed his teeth, ate breakfast, took his lunch box, and ran out to the neighbour's house to pet Toby before he began his day. Then, he would proceed to Ravy's house where Jass and Ravy would be waiting for him. All three of them would walk to school, but some days, he felt confident and would walk by himself to and from school. Bertha and John would also keep an eye out for Manny. He would always wave or sometimes stop by the Smith's to pet Toby after school as well. Bertha would often have some milk and cookies for Manny. He indulged in them as soon as he saw them.

Kuljit discussed putting the boys in soccer. She said to Manjot that it would be good for them to play a sport so they could build a relationship with other kids, and they could also play the game at lunchtime.

Manny loved playing soccer, and when his mother suggested it, he loudly exclaimed "Yes, mom! I really want to."

So, they registered the boys for soccer. They would play on Saturdays, wearing soccer cleats, shin pads, and green striped uniforms. Manny would kick the ball high in the air, while Ravy would try to head-butt it, and the women would watch their boys playing and having fun. They would play a round-robin tournament with six teams. At halftime, all the teams would eat McDonald's cheeseburgers and drink orange pop. Manny and Ravy had fun playing with all the other kids. The boys recognized one kid, Jason. He was in Manny and Ravy's kindergarten class. They all quickly became friends, playing with each other after school and during recess.

Halloween was near, and Ravy bought a costume. Manny wanted to dress up as well. This was his first Halloween in Canada. He got his mother to go out with him to buy him a Dracula costume. He put on the Dracula outfit at home and ran around outside trying to scare Toby, the Smiths, and whoever came by. He even startled Mr. Singh when he came home, and Mr. Singh laughed. The next day, the boys both went to school, all dressed up in their costumes. Manny was so excited he actually slept with his costume on. Manny saw all the kids and teachers dressed up. They had a Halloween party at school with chips, pops, and candy bars. Halloween was a new concept for Manjot. She saw all the kids dressed up and enjoyed how cute they looked. It made her laugh too.

So, Kuljit told her friend to come with her to the store after they dropped off the kids at school and said, "Let's go get candy and chocolate for the kids."

She said Halloween was something like *Diwali*. (This is a Hindu celebration, but many Sikhs celebrate it. It is the festival of lights held between October and November, and sweets are distributed.) Kuljit explained that it was celebrated every year on October 31.

"This is when the little kids, all dressed up, will knock on your door at night and say, 'Trick or treat.' Then, you just give them some candy or chocolate. They will continue to come till about eight o'clock or so. Just make sure that you have enough to give to everybody, and if you don't want to dress up, you don't worry. I will be taking the boys out for trick-or-treating."

During Halloween, neighbourhood children came to the Singh's house for trick-or-treating, and Manjot answered every door knock and gave each of the kids a chocolate bar. She was very impressed at how many kids would come and knock at the door and how cute their costumes were. Mr. Singh was getting a little annoyed.

He said to Manjot, "Are they going to keep coming all night? I have to go to work in the morning, and these kids have to go to school too. When is Manny coming home?"

Manjot said to Mr. Singh, "Shhh! This is only once a year. Let the kids have fun. It is like how we celebrated Diwali in India."

Mr. Singh didn't argue and decided to go to bed. He was thinking that in India, his father never let him go and celebrate.

He confessed to Manjot, "I wish I could have celebrated *Diwali* as a kid," and went to bed.

Late that night, lying in her bed, Manjot was thinking how hard a life Mr. Singh had led in India and felt a little bad for him that he had such tough parents who blamed him for his brother's death. She also remembered how her own father treated her like his princess. Even though he never had a boy, he loved Manjot very much and took her to every *Diwali* celebration and any other celebration that was going on at that time in India. For her birthday, her father bought many gifts and food and invited everyone in the village to celebrate, even though he was not a very wealthy man.

Manny came back with many chocolates and candies. He told his mother about how he went from house to house saying, "Trick or treat," and how all the children were dressed up and walking around at night.

She hugged her boy and said, "Yes, my son. I too had fun giving candy to all the kids that came by knocking on the door. Maybe next year I will dress up too."

Over the next few days, all the children would bring the chocolates and candies to school, eating them during recess.

Two years passed and Manny was loving school. He was to start grade 1. Manjot bought him a brand new bike, since Kuljit had bought one for Ravy too. Manny was excited and rode it every day to school, racing with all of the other kids on their bikes.

One day, it was a little wet and slippery outside, and Manny fell off his bike while returning from school. He landed face-first on the gravel road. He had cuts all over his body. He picked up his bike and walked with it home, crying and cursing at it.

John noticed him, came out, and said, "Manny, did you fall off your bike?"

Manny said, "Yes, I did. I hate this bike."

John cleaned Manny's wounds, put a bandage on his knee, and said, "Look, my boy, in life, you are gonna fall off your bike. I did, everybody does, but you have to get back on your bike and keep riding. The pain will go away, I promise. I know you can do it; you have the heart of a lion. Roar, my boy, roar!"

Despite his tears and pain, Manny got back on his bike and started riding it again. The wind blew his tears into the air, and he did roar like a lion.

By now, Manny had made new friends with whom he connected well, and they lived just up the block. Jason and Manny had been in the same class since kindergarten and played on the same soccer team. He would go over to Jason's house because he had video games. Jason loved sports, so he also played street hockey with Manny and Ravy. The kids would play almost every day into the night until just before supper time. Manny would also move the net to accommodate oncoming traffic. He loved playing goalie.

Lee, another friend who had been in their kindergarten class, lived right beside Jason's house. Lee's parents were poor. They were alcoholics. Sometimes his father would work, and his mother was always out, never home. At times, Lee would come to school with no jacket, barefoot, and wearing the same clothes every day. At lunchtime, Lee would watch all his classmates opening their lunchboxes and eating sandwiches, fruit rolls, peanut butter, cheese and crackers, Ding Dongs, Twinkies, and other treats. Lee watched them with no lunch and stomach growling. He would observe everyone to see who might throw their lunch in the garbage so he could eat the leftovers. Manny observed Lee, who was always by himself, looking through the garbage for food. His schoolmates would make fun of his clothes and bare feet and that he stank all the time from not taking a shower. His hair was never combed and full of dandruff. Manny felt sorry for Lee, thinking about how he was hungry and sad.

One recess, when Manny went to the washroom, he heard someone crying. When Manny went in, he saw Lee coming out with his hands on his stomach, and he looked at Manny on the way out. The next day, Manny grabbed a Ding Dong out of his lunch box and walked over to Lee to give it to him. Lee was too shy to grab it, but Manny told him it was okay and asked him to take it. Since his schoolmates bullied Lee every day, and he didn't know if Manny was sincere or just playing a big trick, Lee slowly grabbed the Ding Dong and devoured the whole thing within seconds. Manny realized that this boy was always hungry but didn't have any lunch. Lee looked gratefully at Manny as if he were the first person to be nice to him.

The next day, Lee tried to sit close to Manny, Ravy, and Jason, feeling welcome and that maybe he had some friends at school, after all.

Jason said to Manny and Ravy, "You guys leave him alone; don't talk to him or give him anything. Do you realize that his parents have no money to feed him?"

Jason told Manny that his mother told him to stay away from Lee because his parents were alcoholics.

Manny said to Jason, "Let's help him at lunchtime. I will bring some extra food like a couple extra Ding Dongs and Twinkies for Lee."

Jason wasn't too sure about this idea since his parents didn't want anything to do with Lee's family, but he was at least able to bring him crackers as Manny had told him to. Ravy would also bring some cookies for him. Manny brought him fruit rolls with an extra ham sandwich and fruit juice. He told his mother that he was really hungry, as an excuse to bring Lee some food, so he wanted more food in his lunch. Manjot became suspicious and thought to herself that maybe the skinny boy that Manny had brought over to the house, who had no shoes on and looked like he never took a shower, was perhaps hungry because when she made roti for them, Lee finished five rotis in no time, while the other kids had only two.

Manjot didn't mind him giving away food because in the Sikh faith it is one of the religious deeds to feed any person who is hungry, regardless of their belief or religion. She got Manny to admit why he was taking such a big lunch. Then, she hugged him and told him she didn't mind packing a little extra lunch if he was giving it to someone hungry. She said that she would start packing a separate lunch for Lee and what Manny was doing was very good and from the heart. She told him that Lee could come over to their house anytime. Manny's face lit up, and he hugged and thanked Manjot. She also gave Lee some clothes that Manny was growing out of and never wore. As for Lee, he never wanted to leave Manny's house every time he came over, and he always wanted to come over.

Manny never said no to Lee or any of his friends if they wanted to visit, regardless of their skin colour, faith, or religion. They were always more than welcome to his house, especially after he heard the stories of Lee's parents fighting at night. Jason would tell him all about it. Manjot knew about it too and insisted they come over to eat. Besides, the Caucasian boys loved Indian food, especially the *samosas,* and would learn some bad words in Punjabi from Manny.

CHAPTER 10

Manny was becoming more and more independent. He had great freedom as a young lad. Manjot's English became very good, and she had gotten herself a driver's licence, so she would go shopping all by herself. All the business owners soon started recognizing Manjot and calling her Mrs. Singh. She felt confident and was well-liked and respected by everyone. As for Mr. Singh, he would slave away six days a week, but during the summer, he would leave home for a few weeks to visit his second cousin in Toronto. He started making this trip annually and eventually purchased a house there.

For Manjot, summertime meant she could have more freedom from Mr. Singh when he was gone to Toronto, but this summer she felt very hurt and scared because of the events happening in India. Mr. Singh stayed longer in Toronto to support the Punjabi community there. His whole family and the Sikh community living across the globe were torn because Sikhs were being slaughtered by the Indian Government. The year 1984 remains one of the darkest in modern Indian history. In June of that year, Prime Minister Indira Gandhi ordered a military assault on the most significant religious centre for the Sikhs, *Darbar Sahib* (the Golden Temple) in Amritsar, Punjab. The attack killed thousands of civilians. On October 31, 1984, Mrs. Gandhi was assassinated by two of her Sikh bodyguards. Her assassination triggered genocidal killings around the country, particularly in India's capital city, New Delhi. *TIME* reported on massacres a day after the violence subsided. Frenzied mobs of young Hindu thugs, thirsty for revenge, burned Sikh-owned stores to the ground, dragged Sikhs out of their homes, cars, and trains, then clubbed them to death or set them aflame before raring off in search of other victims. Witnesses watched with horror as the mobs walked the streets of New Delhi, gang-raping Sikh women, murdering Sikh men, and burning down homes, businesses, and *Gurudwaras* (Sikh houses of worship). Eyewitness accounts describe how law enforcement and government officials participated in the massacres by engaging in the violence, inciting civilians to seek vengeance, and providing the mobs with weapons. The pogroms continued unabated, and according to the official reports, within three days, nearly 3,000 Sikhs had been murdered, at the rate of one per minute. This was the peak of the violence. Unofficial death estimates were far higher, and human rights activists had identified specific individuals complicit in organizing and perpetrating the massacres. Barbara Crossette, a former *New York Times* bureau chief in New Delhi, in a report for *World Policy Journal*, pointed out that almost as many Sikhs died in a few days in India in 1984 as all the deaths and disappearances in Chile during the 17-year military rule of General Augusto Pinochet between 1973 and 1990.

Manjot was very careful about going out that summer and told Manny to come back home before nightfall. She was scared because of what was happening in India, and all the Sikh families stayed in close contact with each other for support. Mr. Singh returned home quickly, wanting to be there to protect his family.

Some years went by, and things started to calm down. Manny was starting grade 6. It was not the same for him because Ravy was not in his class, neither was Jason or Lee, although they had all been in the same class in the previous years.

A month into the new school year, a mentally challenged boy named Ross caught Manny's attention. Manny felt for him. He always said "hi" to him and opened the school doors for him. Ross would appreciate it, even though he couldn't speak. He tried to do so by moaning and clapping his hands. Manny saw Ross being made fun of and felt bad for him. It reminded him of how Lee was treated, and he knew it wasn't right. Manny had a soft spot in his heart for the underdogs or children who were less popular or privileged than the other children. He could relate to them because of his own experiences.

Classmates would throw paper balls at Ross and push him at lunch and call him a "retard." They would imitate him, making the noises he did. Manny never did that, and he would tell the other boys to stop bothering Ross.

A few of the boys had been teasing Manny since the start of the school year, and it quickly escalated. One of the boys, Dirk, was a bully. He kept calling Manny a "poo head" and a "fucking Hindu." Joining him in his antics were Dean and Todd. Dirk was tall and lanky. In class, they would shoot elastic bands at Manny, especially at his turban, and push him around. They would threaten to beat him up. Out of fear, poor, skinny Manny would give Dirk his Ding Dongs and Twinkies and would be scared to come to school. He felt safer only when the bell rang. He went immediately up to Ravy's class down the hallway so he would have someone to go home with and not have to ride by himself. Todd and Dean bullied their peers sometimes, but Dirk was the main perpetrator. He hated Manny and would torture him every day, scaring him by saying that he was going to "cut off his turban and beat him up bad" and by following him at lunchtime.

Ravy knew what Manny was going through every day; after all, they were best friends. He told only Ravy about the bullying because he didn't want to seem like a coward by telling everyone about it.

Ravy said, "I will talk to him, my friend."

Manny was hesitant as he didn't want his friend to get hurt and told him that he didn't have to do that for him. Ravy told Manny that he wasn't scared of Dirk. Manny was shocked to hear that because Ravy was smaller than Manny and much smaller than Dirk. He told Manny he would stop Dirk from tormenting him, but Manny didn't think it was a good idea.

That day after school, Ravy, pretending not to be scared, was very frightened when he walked up to Dirk with Manny and said, "Dirk, stop bugging my friend. Leave him alone."

Dirk walked right up to Ravy and started laughing. He was a foot taller than Ravy.

He said, "What are you gonna do, Smurf?"

Dirk punched Ravy on the side of the head. Ravy went down hard. Manny tried to stop Dirk. He punched Manny in the turban. Todd grabbed Dirk and told him to leave because the teachers might come. Manny helped Ravy up. Ravy had a shiner, and Manny's head hurt slightly. Both of them missed school the next day and were very careful to stay out of Dirk's way. Dirk bullied many of the kids, not just Manny. He tripped Ross, even though he was mentally challenged, and Ross fell on his face and broke his tooth.

Dirk's father was a drunkard who used to hit him with a belt, and his family was poor. He would come to school barefoot. He was a tall, blue-eyed, blond kid who wore ripped jeans and an Iron Maiden T-shirt.

At lunchtime, Dirk came from behind and pushed poor Manny.

Dirk said, "Stand up, Hindu! Stand fucking up!"

Manny stood up finally, and Dirk punched him in the eye. He fell to the ground, then Dirk kicked him and pulled off his red bun turban. All of a sudden, the crowd watching the fight scattered, including Dean and Todd.

Ravy picked Manny up and said, "Let's go!"

The teachers came outside and helped Manny back to the principal's office to find out what happened. They were not surprised at all. The principal already knew that Dirk was a bully. Dirk was suspended for three days, and they immediately moved Manny to Ravy's class. They also called in Manny's parents.

Manjot came to see the principal at school the next day, and they told her that Dirk was bullying Manny and other children, and if it ever happened again, the school would take further disciplinary action. The principal also mentioned that Dirk came from a bad home and was abused by his alcoholic father. He apologized to Manjot.

For weeks, Manny would lie in bed at night and wish he looked different, maybe Caucasian, even if just for a day. He wanted to be accepted and not feel different. He even thought of cutting his turban off so that nobody would make fun of him or his skin colour any longer. He felt out of place for the first time because he was a bit older now and understood what was going on. When he was younger, children played with each other regardless of how they looked and what religion they followed.

Manny confronted his mother and told her that he wanted to get a haircut and not wear a turban anymore, like Ravy. Manjot was upset about the whole situation and how her son felt. She could feel her son's pain when he expressed wanting to cut his hair.

She knew the bullying was racially motivated and felt the principal wasn't handling the situation appropriately.

Manjot hugged her son and said, "Don't worry, my son. I know you want to fit in. It's hard, but your father would never agree for you to cut your hair, and people just don't know why you wear your turban. It represents our faith, culture, and religion. You will be okay, son. Dirk will not bully you anymore."

Since Manny did not go to school for a week after the bullying incident, Jason and Lee went over to Manny's house, apologizing that they had not been there to help him. They assured Manny that they were going to protect him and not let Dirk bully him anymore. Jason insisted that he should fight Dirk and try to beat him up since he was a strong kid for his age. Manny felt good about his friends supporting him.

A week later, Manjot accompanied him to school, and he felt secure in the class with his friends, Jason, Lee, and Ravy. The four of them hung out as a mini-gang at lunch and made a pact to protect each other.

Lee told Manny that he would fight Dirk because of what he did, but Manny said to Lee, "I don't want to get you in trouble, but thanks."

Jason also said Dirk wouldn't dare to do anything if they all stuck together.

CHAPTER 11

A few months had passed. Dirk seemed to have left Manny alone, except for an incident one weekend. Ravy and Manny were riding their bikes through a trail on the other side of the town and ran into Dirk and his friends. Filled with fear, Manny immediately braked. They tried to turn around but crashed.

Dirk said to Dean, "Let's get them!"

They all surrounded Manny and Ravy. They were pushing Manny around, calling him "poo head" and asking mockingly, "What's that weird thing on your head?"

Manny was so frightened that he ran away, leaving his bike. The bullies picked up his bike and smashed it to the ground. Ravy picked up Manny to take him on his bike to get away from the boys. But the bullies didn't bother chasing them; they just took off. When Ravy and Manny went back to get his bike, they saw it was broken. Dirk and his friends were looking on from a distance, laughing out loud and calling Manny names, such as "cry baby." Manny was very sad and upset. He cried all the way home with his broken bike.

Mr. Singh yelled at Manny and told him he was stupid for riding to the other side of town and to stay on his street. He said

Ravy was a bad influence. He also said he should have never gotten him the bike.

John overheard the yelling. He looked at the mangled bike, grabbed it, and took it over to his garage. Manny followed John to his place, struggling to catch his breath after crying. John looked at Manny's face and saw that the little boy was heartbroken. It made John feel sad. He assured Manny he would fix his bike for him.

He gave him a lollipop and said, "You watch me work on your bike. I will show you how to put the chain back on the bike and tighten the wheels."

Then he stood the bike up and said, "Taadaaah! I fixed it."

John gave Manny a big hug and took his bike over to his house.

That night, Manny took a long look at himself in the mirror, feeling his turban and thinking of himself as an outcast. As he thought of the bullying, tears fell from his eyes as he tried to understand the reason why he was a target. It hurt him so deeply inside. In the morning, the dried tears showed on his eyelids.

He dreamed that John was his father, as he could never show emotion or communicate with his real father. Mr. Singh would hardly show any interest in or emotion towards the young man. He tried only to discipline him with criticism and harsh rules. Manny truly enjoyed the time he spent with John. Not only did John show him how to fix things, but he was also a generous man who paid attention to the boy. He didn't criticize him but instead played with him and treated him well. At times, when Manny was upset with his father, he would wander off to John's and would think about how different things would be if John were his actual father instead of Mr. Singh, since he considered John a role model. John and Bertha never had a son. They had two daughters, who were married and lived on the mainland. John felt Manny was the closest thing he'd ever had to a son.

A few weeks later, Toby passed away. He was quite an old dog. Manny was very sad for about two weeks and kept quiet, remembering how he used to play with the dog before and after school. Mr. Singh noticed and asked Manjot what was wrong with Manny and why he wasn't talking like his usual self. She explained that he was sad the dog next door died because he was emotionally attached to it.

Mr. Singh laughed and went into Manny's room.

He said, "Don't be a wussy. Why crying over a dog?" and grabbed his ear.

Manny grabbed Mr. Singh's hand and said, "Don't touch me!"

Mr. Singh was shocked. Manny had never had this angry reaction before.

Mr. Singh said, "You're a big man, hey. You think you're a big kid now? Maybe go live with your friends?"

Mr. Singh went to his room thinking to himself that his son was starting to become a young man with a bad attitude who didn't know any better and didn't realize that it was he (Mr. Singh) who provided for the family.

Another year had passed, and Manny was still getting bullied by Dirk. However, one day, he decided to start fighting back at Dirk. As he had never seen anybody challenge him before, Dirk didn't like it at all.

Manny said, "Let's meet at the school on Saturday at 1 p.m. I want to fight you."

Manny had this look in his eyes as if he didn't care about Dirk. He was full of anger and ready to lash out. Dirk looked puzzled and shocked that Manny wanted to fight him.

He could only utter, "Oookayyy! See you on Saturday."

Dirk didn't say anything to Manny for the rest of the week. Finally, it was Saturday, and Dirk, Todd, and Dean were waiting at the designated place, anticipating "kicking Manny's ass and kicking it good." Then the gang of Manny, Ravy, Jason, and Lee arrived. Behind them, were two big Indian fellows who were Ravy's older cousins from the mainland. They must have been at least three years older than the other boys. Dean and Todd got scared and took off. Dirk was standing there, scared but pretending not to be.

Manny said, "Let's fight!"

He punched Dirk, and Dirk punched him back. Manny fell to the ground, taking Dirk with him. Manny put Dirk in a head lock, and then all of them ganged up on Dirk. Ravy's older cousins started punching Dirk, while Ravy started kicking Dirk. He was on the ground, curled up like a ball, and they kept kicking him and then left him there.

Manny said to Dirk, "Don't mess with us again, or else we will beat you up some more."

Dirk was curled up and crying on the ground.

After that day, Dirk and his gang never looked at Manny and Ravy again and stayed clear of them. The four horsemen, Manny, Ravy, Jason, and Lee were practically in charge of the school because everyone had heard about what had happened on the weekend. Everyone in school was treating them differently. They were like superheroes to all the other kids being bullied by Dirk. They had become the popular kids, and Manny wasn't scared anymore. He was ready to fight Dirk any time and stand up for anyone being bulled, and everyone knew it.

A week went by, and Manny and Manjot went shopping for a new backpack after school. On the way, he saw the cutest little puppy in a pet store. It reminded him of Toby. He wanted it very much and begged his mother to get it. He said he would do any-thing to get the little puppy. Manjot thought the look in Manny's eye when he saw this puppy was so adorable; it was instant love. Manjot had seen that same look before when he was very young and saw Toby for the first time.

She said, "We have to ask your dad first. Maybe he will not allow it."

Manny's face fell, and Manjot felt conflicted because he wanted this puppy so badly.

Manny waited impatiently for his father to come home and said, "*Papa, main doggy lana*." (Dad, I want a dog.)

Mr. Singh said, "Son, wait till you're a bit older. I'll get you one."

Mr. Singh was thinking he would never get him one and was trying to be kind at that moment because he knew how much his son loved dogs and had seen what an impact Toby had on him.

Manny left with a sad face. Manjot saw the sadness in her son's eyes and tried to convince Mr. Singh that he very much wanted a puppy and he was old enough now to take care of a dog. Mr. Singh couldn't understand why he wanted a dog so much, because in India, the dogs were strays and wild, and nobody took them in. He felt his son was being a "wussy" for wanting a dog. It didn't make any sense to Mr. Singh.

Every day for six months Manny asked his parents for a dog. Mr. Singh ignored him. Finally, on his birthday in the summer, as it was his last year in elementary school, Manjot went to the pet shop and bought him a puppy without Mr. Singh's knowledge when he was away in Toronto. She surprised him by bringing the puppy into his room. He was ecstatic and hugged his mother.

He said, "This is the best birthday present that I could ever have."

Manny was so excited. He picked up the puppy and went to show the Smiths.

John said, "Well, well, well, what do we have here? It's such a cute puppy."

Manny said, "Yes he is. I'm going to call him Rocky."

"That is a really nice name," John said.

Manny was so excited to show everyone his new pet that he abruptly left John's house and ran to Ravy's house with Rocky. Ravy was excited too. The boys tried to play fetch with the puppy, but all he did was nibble and lick their faces. After a few hours of playing at Ravy's, Manny brought Rocky back home so he could feed him. The German Shepherd started eating dog food as he was very hungry.

Manny had to pick up the puppy's poop every day. Manjot would never have to remind him to do it because he loved Rocky very much. Manny kept Rocky in his room and slept with him by his side. The summer heat would sometimes cause him to put Rocky in the garage, where it was cool at nighttime. Ravy and Manny would play with Rocky all day long, never leaving him out of their sight.

Mr. Singh was about to come back home in a few days, and Manjot told Manny, "Keep Rocky in the backyard for now. When Papa comes back home, we will tell him about Rocky."

When Manjot told Mr. Singh about Rocky, he was upset, but Manjot convinced Mr. Singh that she felt unsafe with nobody at the house, and Rocky would be a good guard dog. She said burglars would break into the house with them both working and Manny going back to school. Rocky would be in the backyard and not bother him.

Grade 7 was the last year of elementary school, so the grade 7 students felt like the kings and queens of their school because they were the most senior students. Manny and Ravy were considered the ultimate "cool dudes," who would joke in class. Manny now sported a light moustache and had a growth spurt over the summer. He grew more than a foot, but Ravy grew only two inches.

At that age, boys and girls start liking each other. Later in the year, at the school dance, Manny danced with girls and held their hands. He felt tingly in his body and liked the feeling. His hormones were raging, but he still acted very shyly towards any girl. They would ask him out, and he wouldn't know what to say and run away. He started having wet dreams. By the end of the year, his voice started breaking. He was going through the changes of puberty. He was becoming a man.

CHAPTER 12

It was Sports Day at the end of the elementary school year, and Manny came in first place in every event. He was a track and field star. He threw the shot put as if it were a baseball, and it went high and far. The discus was like a frisbee; it didn't take much effort before it was long and gone. As for the high jump, with his lanky legs and big feet, it seemed Manny could leap buildings like Superman. His height from his growth spurt made him one of the best. When he ran the 100-metre dash and 4x4 relay event, his lean physique and muscular body gave him a competitive edge. He was like a cheetah out of the gate; he ran so fast and left all the other competitors behind in the dust and was the first one to cross the finish line. He broke almost all school records and was rewarded for his sportsmanship and excellence with ribbons and trophies.

One day in late June, near the end of the school year, Manny and Ravy skipped school and went back to Ravy's house. Nobody was home. The boys decided to try one of Harry's cigarettes. They went outside to the backyard and tried smoking. Manny took the cigarette, put it in his mouth, tried to light it, but it didn't work. After a few tries, he finally lit it from the match. He put the cigarette in his mouth, took a puff, felt the strong smoke in his throat, and immediately started coughing. He handed it to Ravy so he could have a puff, and the same thing happened to him.

Manny told Ravy that he was going to go back inside to grab some water to clear his throat and accidentally went into Jass' room. He saw her pink G-string and bra there. He picked up the underwear gently out of curiosity. He began to smell the underwear and bra and became aroused by the thought of her wearing them. He started imagining her naked. Then, he heard the door open and saw Ravy come back inside the house, coughing loudly. Manny quickly shot out of Jass' room. Ravy didn't notice that Manny had been in his sister's room but noticed that her door was wide open, so he shut it. Then, he asked Manny how he liked the cigarette. Manny said that he would not try to smoke again because it burnt his lungs and throat. Ravy said that he liked the feeling and had another puff.

He kept coughing but said, "After a few cigs, it doesn't hurt anymore, my friend."

Manny laughed at Ravy, put him in a headlock, and took him outside the house.

The boys tried to smoke again, but this time, someone else opened the door. They quickly tried to put out the cigarette. Jass was standing there, all dolled up wearing a denim skirt. Her brown, silky legs were showing all the way up to the top of her thighs, and her small tank top showed her cleavage. Her red high heels made her look much taller than she was. She wore makeup and eyeliner, which emphasized her lips and big brown eyes. Her hair was long and curly. She told Ravy she saw what they were doing and warned them not to smoke again. Manny noticed himself paying attention to Jass' looks. In all the years of going over to the house, he never thought of Jass as someone he liked but more like a big sister. Now that she looked like Tina Turner, she made him drool and his eyes pop out of his head. Maybe puberty had something to do with it. Manny's hormones were out of control along with his zits. His first teenage crush was his friend's older sister!

Manny kept it to himself, but Jass did notice him acting strangely around her and his brown face turning red. He also behaved shyly towards her, which never used to happen before. She knew why. Someone had been in her room snooping around her panties and bra. She had always kept them folded together, but this time, they were on opposite sides of the room. She didn't mention the incident to anyone at the time but assumed that Manny had been in her room. She told only her close friends about it.

Her friend thought it was cute that this young kid had a crush on her and teased her saying, "Take your younger brother's friend out to prom. Maybe he can bring you on a tricycle."

Jass told her friends to be quiet, while she giggled away. Ravy had no clue what was going on; he hadn't yet reached puberty.

Over the years, since Manny had been interested in cars from a very young age, and John was a retired mechanic, he would occasionally teach Manny the basics about cars—where the battery was or where to check the engine oil. During that summer, now that he was a teenager, his curiosity about everything related to the engine grew. He asked John to teach him everything there was to know about cars, trucks, and motorbikes, and of course, John agreed. He saw Manny's passion, and Manny reminded John of himself at that age. From early in the morning, Manny would work on John's older vehicles that were sitting in his garage. The two of them would spend countless hours fixing up old cars, and by the end of the day, oil would be all over Manny's overalls, face, and hair. Then, they would grab a snack that Bertha had made for them. They would both sit down and talk about how John had a passion for cars like Manny did at his age and whatever else was going on in young Manny's life. Manny was open and straightforward with John.

He felt as if he could tell him anything and said, "John, I thank you so much for teaching me and spending time with me. You are like a father to me. I genuinely thank you and Bertha."

John said, "No problem! You are like the son I never had. I just want the best for you, and you can tell me anything in the world. If you need anything, Bertha and I are here for you."

A teardrop fell from John's eye. Manny wiped it with his greasy hand and gave John a big hug.

Mr. Singh was a bit jealous of John because his son would tell Manjot about how he loved working on cars and would never be around the house anymore when Mr. Singh came home from work. Manjot told Mr. Singh what Manny was doing, and he overheard their conversation about how great John was to him. Mr. Singh suggested that Manny didn't need to spend that much time with John, especially because he was old and white.

Manjot looked at Mr. Singh and said, "Our son wants to be a mechanic, and John is teaching him. That is his passion; he loves what he is doing. So, let him learn. I think it is good for him." Mr. Singh looked at Manjot and said, "See, I would rather want him to be a doctor or lawyer. How can he become a mechanic when he has no idea how to fix anything? I think he is just wasting his time with that *bouddha*."

Manjot went into her bedroom without saying anything to Mr. Singh, as she always did.

He was worried his son was going to get too close to John, so he tried talking to Manny about it, and Manny looked him straight in the eyes and said, "Papa, I want to be a mechanic."

Mr. Singh did not react. He went into his bedroom, not saying anything to Manny.

It was a nice hot summer. Manny was a busy teenager. In the evenings, he and Ravy would take Rocky with them for bike rides to the corner store to grab some Slurpees, candies, and bubble gum. They would race each other, and whoever came first would have to buy the other one the Slurpee. Manny would win almost all the time, and they would tie Rocky up outside the store. The boys rode all around town into the wee hours of the night and sometimes would ride on the bike trails. It was where all the kids hung out and brought their dogs during summer. Some days, the boys loved to play video games. Manny finally got his very own Atari video game system, and he would play often with Ravy.

After summer, the new session of school would begin. The boys would go to junior high school and start grade 8. On the first day of junior high, Manjot drove Manny and Ravy to the new school. It was much farther away than their elementary school had been. This one was about 10 minutes across town and close to the highway.

Manjot pulled up in front of the school and said, "Here you go, boys!"

Manny asked, "Will you be picking us up or will Aunty Kuljit?"

"I'll be here at 12, okay?"

"Okay, mom! Love you, bye!"

Manny was smiling. He had grown a few more inches during that summer. He was prescribed reading glasses, so he wore them with his black turban bun and new Levi's jean and dress shirt. Ravy was wearing jeans and a buttoned-up shirt. The boys proceeded to their assigned classrooms and hoped they would be together in the same class.

"Wow," thought Manny, "I've never seen so many different kids, and I don't recognize any of them from elementary school."

The students were from different elementary schools around the area and another smaller community beside his town that didn't have a junior high school. So many strange faces filled Manny with anxiety.

The first few days, everyone was settling into their new classrooms and exploring the surroundings to understand the layout of the school. Everyone was assigned their own locker. Ravy's locker was upstairs, and Manny's was downstairs. Manny asked Ravy to ask if the student next to Ravy wanted to switch lockers with him, so they could be beside each other.

Ravy said, "Okay, my bro! I will."

The bell rang, and the boys had to go to their classes.

CHAPTER 13

Manny had English class near his locker, and Ravy had Math class on the other side of the school. Manny's teacher introduced herself as Mrs. Oryan. Manny sat down with his big binder and black reading glasses and noticed a stunning girl sitting right beside him. She had gorgeous green eyes with auburn hair and a big smile. Immediately, Manny felt a familiar impulse, and his body temperature began to rise. He was looking at her, spellbound, and when she looked back at him and smiled, he turned his head directly forward and pretended that he wasn't looking at her. His little brown face became red and he clutched his legs together.

Manny thought, "I'm getting a boner," and he didn't want anyone to see it.

He became infatuated with this girl, and his attention was solely on her. The teacher's lessons would go in one ear and out the other.

As the bell went, the class ended, and the girl turned around to Manny and said, "Hi, my name is Crystal. Nice to meet you."

Manny mumbled, "Manny, name."

He was so nervous, he just froze. Crystal got up to go to the next class as did all the other students. Manny was the last one to leave the class. He was mesmerized and slowly got up from his desk. With his mind fixated on this beautiful girl, he proceeded to his locker. Then, he noticed the girl he was just talking to. Her locker was right next to his. He couldn't believe it. He was too shy to go up to his locker because she was right there. He watched her leave, and then he went to his locker. As he walked by her, he smelled her perfume and tried to quickly open his locker as if he didn't notice. She smiled and said goodbye. As she left for her class, Manny's hormones were through the roof, and his jaw dropped. He had a huge crush on this girl. He couldn't believe she talked to him and kept thinking about her for the rest of the day.

As the day ended, Ravy came up to Manny and said, "Yo, bro! The *gora* will switch locker with you so you can be beside me, okay?"

Manny said, "No, I can't, bro. My class is closer to my locker."

Ravy was shocked to hear what his friend was saying and asked him if he was feeling okay. Ravy noticed that Manny looked a little dazed, as if he were sleepwalking.

The next day, when his mother dropped them both off at school, he noticed Crystal looking at him as he was getting out of his mother's car and felt a little embarrassed. From the next day onwards, he made his mother drop him off, not in front of the school anymore, but near the school on the corner of the street. His mother assumed that he was at an age when he wanted to be cool and not be dropped off by his mother. She knew he was growing up, so she didn't ask him to explain the reason. She just smiled about it. Ravy was puzzled about why Manny wanted to be dropped off away from the school. To him, walking a greater distance to the school didn't make sense. Manny didn't want to tell anybody that he had a crush on Crystal, so as an excuse, he told Ravy and his mother that his teacher advised him to get fresh air and observe the new school and people.

Manny would always be sitting in English class early, hoping Crystal would come early as well. Then, when Crystal would come into the class, he would first smell her perfume. He was in love with her and held his breath and felt tingling in his body whenever Crystal looked at him or sat beside him. They were together in two classes, physical education and English.

A month later, Manny still had a big crush on Crystal. He was acting differently towards his mother, Ravy, and even the Smiths. He was more distant, couldn't sleep at night, and kept thinking about Crystal all day and night. Ravy hadn't yet reached puberty, so he didn't understand the reason behind Manny's strange behaviour and was puzzled as to why Manny's demeanour was changing and he did not want to play with Ravy anymore the way they used to.

Manny was masturbating one night in his room on top of the covers when Mr. Singh opened the door and walked straight in without knocking. Manny was shocked because his father never ever used to come into his room. His underwear was down, and his hands were on his penis. He immediately pulled his underwear up.

Mr. Singh said, "*sala,*" and grabbed him by his ear but let go when Manny clutched his hand. There was a brief silence between them. Manny's face turned red. Mr. Singh told Manny to take out the garbage cans on the morning of every second Thursday from then on because he was old enough to do it. Then, Mr. Singh left Manny's room, shaking his head in disappointment, and closed the door behind him. Manny exhaled and put his bed covers back on. He realized that it wasn't a smart idea to try masturbating with Mr. Singh around.

It was late September when Manny and Ravy joined the basketball team. His practice sessions were after school until about 4:30 p.m., and then Manjot or Kuljit would pick them up. Mr. Singh was still strict. Manny was not allowed to go anywhere after school except for his basketball practice sessions, and he had to study for extra hours. Mr. Singh wanted him to get good grades, so he had to study hard.

One Thursday afternoon at practice, the boys were shooting baskets when a few girls from their class came to the stands to watch them. Manny couldn't believe Crystal was there too. He started to show off by trying three-point shots farther away from the rim and pretended to jump and dunk the ball. The young ladies watched the boys, and Crystal smiled at Manny. Manny was so happy to see her that he put in extra effort and played harder at the practice.

A few days later, there was a home opener. For the boys, it was the beginning of the new basketball season. Before the game was about to start, Manny noticed Crystal again, wearing a beautiful blouse with big, black sandals. She was sitting with a couple of her friends.

Ravy noticed Manny gawking at Crystal and said, "Hmm, so that is her! You like that girl. She has her locker right next to you, and that's why you didn't want to move. *Haye!*"

Manny did not respond and began focussing on the game. Manny played an excellent game, scoring 25 points as Crystal was cheering him on. They won the game. As he was leaving the court, Crystal stood up and blew a kiss to him from the stands. He became excited and again felt he was falling deeply in love with her. The next day, before class started, Manny noticed that Crystal was smiling and talking to another boy. He was standing near her locker, and he felt a knot in his stomach and a knife through his heart. He didn't go near Crystal and tried to avoid her. She waved and smiled at Manny from a distance, and he pretended to ignore her. He waited until after she went away to go to his locker. He was very upset, and English class was the next class. Manny didn't look happy, and when Crystal said, "Hi Manny," he didn't respond. She was wondering why Manny was acting a bit strangely and not talking to her.

It took a few days for Manny to assess his feelings and realize he had missed Crystal during this time. He felt miserable not talking to Crystal and had to talk to her somehow. Then it happened.

In the next English class, Crystal wrote a note to Manny asking whether he would be her date at the school dance. She wrote X's and O's all over the note.

Manny turned around to her and said, "Yes I will."

As the bell rang, Manny was so happy that he was jumping around. His confidence soared, and he had an extra spring in his step. Again, Ravy noticed a change in his friend's mood from sad and grumpy to happy-go-lucky.

The following day, Crystal asked Manny, "Wanna hang out at lunch? I would really like that."

Manny couldn't believe that this was happening and immediately said, "Yes." He was nervous and excited. His palms were sweaty, and his pulse was racing as they both went to lunch. Walking together, all he was aware of was her perfume smelling so fragrant and lovely, as usual.

At lunchtime, Ravy waited for Manny at his locker. They always spent lunch together, but today, Manny was not to be found. Ravy went from class to class looking for Manny.

Manny and Crystal were sitting outside, underneath a tree. Crystal asked Manny questions, such as where he was from and what elementary school he attended. And then, suddenly, she grabbed his hand and held it. Manny's palm was sweaty. The front of his black turban was sweaty too. He was exhilarated.

After lunch, Crystal said, "I want you to be my boyfriend, and I can be your girlfriend."

Manny jumped with joy and said, "Yes!"

On the way home from school, Ravy asked Manny where he had been at lunchtime and that he'd been looking all over for him but couldn't find him.

Manjot was overhearing the conversation, so Manny said, "Nowhere. Just studying," brushing Ravy off.

Ravy said, "Bro, I'm coming over to your house for a bit."

Manny said, "I'm pretty busy today. I have a lot of school work."

Ravy was surprised and sad that his good friend was telling him he was busy.

Manjot noticed Ravy's long face in the mirror and said, "You can come over Ravy. You don't need to ask Manny."

Ravy smiled, and Manny said, "Okay, come over, my pal!"

The boys were downstairs at Manny's house, and Ravy asked Manny, "What's wrong with you? You don't want to hang out with me anymore. What's the reason? This has been happening for a few weeks. I am your friend. Tell me what's going on."

Manny knew it was time to explain the situation to Ravy because he was his best friend, even if he wouldn't fully understand. Manny told Ravy how he liked this girl, the one who had the locker beside him.

"The really pretty one?" asked Ravy, somewhat jealous that his friend was spending time with this girl instead of him.

Then he told Manny that he liked girls too and asked him to find him one. Manny used to think Ravy still hadn't reached puberty and wouldn't understand that he liked girls, but he was wrong. Ravy was experiencing puberty too and liked girls, just like Manny.

Once the boys had expressed their feelings about how they felt about girls, they would discuss how they both had started to grow hair on their private parts and armpits, the wet dreams they had at night, and how their voices were changing. These changes were on their mind all the time. Puberty was something new to them and extremely exciting, as they were transforming from boys into men.

That Friday, Ravy came over to Manny's house. No one else was there, and the boys started playing video games. Then Ravi said he had a surprise for Manny and showed him a *Playboy* magazine. The boys, very curious, opened the magazine and became very excited looking at the nude photos. Ravy was mentally processing every picture, and Manny also marvelled at the different types of bodies that were in the magazine. The boys were in heaven, their minds in a very different place after secretly looking at the magazine.

Manny asked Ravy, "Next Friday is the dance. How can we get out of the house?"

Ravy said, "I have a great idea. We can say we have a basketball game that evening."

Manny said, "Perfect, bro! Let's make that plan. It sounds awesome."

During the week leading up to the dance, Crystal and Manny went everywhere together. Manny arranged for Crystal's best friend, Tina, to go to the dance with Ravy, so the four of them would double date. The boys requested not to be driven to school anymore or be picked up by their parents. The reason was simple: They walked their girlfriends to and from home and school. They had told their parents that they wanted to get exercise and the coach asked them to walk.

It was Friday, and Manny bought a new pair of black dress pants and shoes with a white dress shirt. He had bought a new bottle of deodorant and cologne. Ravy was also dressed up when he went over to Manny's house.

Manjot looked at the boys, "*Balle* (Wow)! You guys look very dressed up to go to the basketball game."

"Yes, we are, mom. It's a special game. The coach requested this for the dress code."

Kuljit came over to the house and said to Manjot, "Look at our babies. They used to play with G.I. Joes and water guns, and now they are growing up so fast."

Manjot smiled and laughed. John and Bertha saw the boys all dressed up and gave the thumbs-up through the window. John had started using a cane by now and wasn't mobile without its support.

He said, "Have a good time, boys. Stay safe," through his window.

Manjot asked the boys, "Do you need a ride to the game?"

They said, "Yes, mom, please."

So, the boys got dropped off at the school, and shortly after, they walked to the nearby store. Manny bought Crystal the most beautiful and freshest red roses. He paid extra for the florist to write a note with them saying, "You are my shining star. I see through you day and night."

Ravy tried to copy Manny by buying flowers, but he purchased cheap ones with no note for Tina. Then, the cool dudes walked over to Crystal's house to pick her up. Manny knocked on the door, and Crystal appeared. Tina was in the background. Crystal was wearing the most beautiful red dress with black leather high heels. She carried a brand new purse against which shone her long, red nails. Her hair was curled, and her shiny lip gloss and mascara emphasized her lips and thick, black eyelashes. Her perfume smelled like nectar. Manny recognized the beautiful and unique scent from the first day of English class. He was beside himself after seeing how stunning Crystal looked. She adored the flowers. Her face lit up, and she kissed Manny on the cheek.

She said, "Manny, thank you for the flowers. They are so beautiful. I love them so much, and you look so handsome in your outfit."

Manny said, "Crystal you look so amazing yourself. You are looking very elegant."

Crystal took the flowers to the room and read the note Manny had written. She kissed the note and put it somewhere safe in her closet.

The couples walked to the dance. At the first slow song, Crystal grabbed Manny's hands, and they began to dance. They were so close that both of them felt the warmth of each other's bodies. They thought the chemistry was made in heaven. A long kiss happened, Manny's first. He had never had such a euphoric feeling—like fireworks. Her soft lips felt so good on Manny's lips.

Ravy and Tina were also dancing just a few feet apart from them, and he saw Manny kiss Crystal, so Ravy also tried to kiss Tina. But Tina pulled her head away as soon as Ravy stuck out his tongue. Tina put her hand on his mouth and kept it there like a muzzle.

Then, the boy who had been at the locker talking to Crystal was walking towards them. Manny recognized him.

He started to call Manny "a fucking Hindu," as he approached the couple, and said, "Go back to where you came from. You don't belong here turban curry fucker."

Crystal said, "Chris, I don't like you or want to be with you, sorry. Please leave us alone. I already told you Manny and I are going out together."

Chris said, "No, I'm not leaving. How can you possibly go out with a Paki, fucking turbanator? Or you must be a Hindu Humper. Go right ahead."

Chris looked at Manny and continued, "What the fuck is on your fucking head? Looks like a diaper. Hey pussy!" and gave Manny a slight push.

Manny grabbed Chris's legs, and the boys started fighting. They were both on the ground. Manny punched Chris's face and ribs. Ravy stood behind his friend to make sure nobody else would jump in. The music stopped, and the lights came back on. Everybody stopped dancing, and the teachers stepped in. Both boys were suspended immediately and told to see the principal in a few days. Crystal started crying and left for home with Tina right away. She didn't like what had happened. Ravy stayed behind to help and support Manny. Manny and Ravy had to call their mothers to pick them up because the teacher made them wait in the principal's office.

After 15 minutes, Mr. Singh pulled up. Manny was surprised to see his father because he never came to pick up Manny or even drop him off at school. He never had anything to do with his school; it was always his mother's responsibility. The boys hopped in the van and looked a bit nervous because Mr. Singh was there.

Ravy tried to say "*Sat Shri Akaal*, Uncle."

Mr. Singh didn't reply, was very silent, and drove very fast. He dropped Ravy off and then drove Manny home. Manny got out of Mr. Singh's van and started walking towards the front door of the house. Mr. Singh grabbed Manny by his neck from behind and directed him down into the basement.

He said, "You think you are a big fighter, yes?"

Manny looked at Mr. Singh and said, "Papa, he started it."

Mr. Singh slapped Manny very hard two or three times, grabbed his neck, threw him into the closet, and said, "Teacher told me you guys go to dance. You said you had a basketball game, *panchod*. Do you think I am stupid?"

Manjot came running down, held Mr. Singh's arm, and said, "Please don't hit him anymore! Please don't!"

He shrugged off Manjot, and she fell to the ground.

She said, "He is older now. Please, I beg you! Please, I beg you!"

Mr. Singh paused with his hand in the air, as if he was going to slap Manny again but slowly put his hand down and walked out into the other room. Poor Manny still had his hands up anticipating his father was going to hit him. As his father left, Manny called him to come back and "do something about it." He said to his father that he didn't deserve to be his father. He was yelling at the top of his lungs and told him that he was not a good father. Mr. Singh heard everything as he was going to his room but didn't go back to Manny. He felt a little hurt by what Manny said.

Meanwhile, his mother rubbed Manny's hands, and he felt the tears falling from his eyes.

She said, "My little handsome boy, my little handsome boy."

He came close to Manjot and rested his face on her shoulder, weeping. She started to comfort him with soothing words.

The next day, Manny was at home due to the suspension and wasn't allowed back at school till it was over. Mr. Singh came back from work and sat down to eat his supper. Then he started grumbling to Manjot, saying she always took Manny's side and didn't pay any attention to what he did at school.

He said, "Manny gets away with a lot of things. He is spoiled because he spends time with Ravy."

Manjot had enough. She finally confronted Mr. Singh and stood up for herself and her boy. "How about you pay attention to your son? All you do is work, work, work. You never have time for any of us, and yes, he is a young boy. He is gonna have many different life experiences like even going to a dance. Don't you ever do what you did, again."

She grabbed a roll of paper towel and threw it at Mr. Singh.

Manjot said, "All my life, me and my boy put up with you abusing us instead of loving us. Why did you come to Canada? You should have stayed in India if you don't like this and don't like that? What do you like? What do you love?"

She kept screaming and yelling, grabbing the dishes and throwing them on the ground, breaking them.

She went up to Mr. Singh, slapped his chest with her hands, enraged and out of control, beating down on him saying, "Hit me! Kill me!"

He grabbed her arms and held them gently pointing towards the floor. Mr. Singh paused, looked at his bedroom door, let go of the hands, and went inside, not uttering a word. He was thinking that Manjot had become a different woman, but he kept it to himself. Manny was surprised that his mother had something to say after all these years and was happy to see his mother finally stand up to his father, but it was not the first time that she stood up for Manny. Manjot was not afraid of her husband and constantly reminded him of when they did leave him alone for a month after that big fight years ago. Mr. Singh was getting older. Now, he didn't have the energy to fight and be aggressive.

The third and final day of Manny's suspension had passed, and he was missing Crystal immensely. He thought about her all the time and was excited to go back to school. Before class, Manjot and Manny had a meeting with the principal. He told Manny not to fight again and that he would be suspended for a longer time if he did it again. He also said that Chris and Manny should stay away from each other.

At lunchtime, the lovebirds reconnected. They were kissing and couldn't keep their hands off each other. They started spending all their time together and even tried to see each other during the weekends and evenings. Manny would try to sneak out of the window to meet up with Crystal. They were practically inseparable.

After a few months, on Valentine's Day, Manny bought Crystal gifts, flowers, and chocolates. They passionately made love to each other for the very first time at Crystal's house. They lost their virginity to each other and felt even more deeply in love and as if they had been reborn. Everyone in the junior high knew that they were a couple. Chris was still very jealous of their relationship and tried to start rumours about how bad Manny was and tried to do everything possible from a distance to destroy their relationship. He still tried to be in contact with Crystal by saying hi to her now and then.

Ravy and Tina's relationship didn't last very long after the dance. Maybe Tina just dated him because Crystal asked her to as he was Manny's good friend. But they didn't seem to click. It didn't help that Ravy tried to shove his tongue down Tina's throat every time he saw her.

CHAPTER 14

Ravy started to hang out with a different, older crowd of people who were up to no good. Ravy started smoking all the time and experimented with drinking. His new friends were Caucasian or Native, and older females hung out with them all the time. Ravy, being younger and wanting to have friends, thought it was cool to be a part of their group.

The summer had arrived, but this time it was going to be different because Manny had a girlfriend, and her parents were never home. So, his days would be spent at Crystal's house. They would make love all day and watch movies till her parents were about to come back from work. Then, Manny darted out of there, right before they came home. The lovebirds would also have a special spot high in the mountains where they would go because of the view. They would lie down on blankets, waiting for the sunset. Then, they would hold on to each other's hands, all cuddled up, to see the big, bright yellow stars and beautiful sky.

Manny would often say to Crystal, looking into her sparkling eyes, "You are my shining star, day and night, my love."

The summer quickly flew, and they were more in love than ever as the new school year approached. They were in just about every class together and helped each other study to earn good grades. Manny wasn't as smart as Crystal. He got average grades, but Crystal got straight A's and was an honour-roll student.

Thanksgiving was near, and Crystal thought it would be an excellent idea to finally have Manny meet her parents. The time was right to tell her parents that they had been going out for a while, and she didn't want to keep it a secret anymore.

So, one week later, Crystal said to her mother, "Mom, I've been keeping a secret from you, and I want you to know something."

Crystal's mother, Dorothy, replied, "Yes, darling, you can tell me anything."

"Mom, I have a boyfriend."

Dorothy replied, "I knew it! I knew you had a boyfriend. You had a different look and feel to you like you were in love. I noticed it but I also thought you were a normal teenage girl that was moody sometimes and having boy problems. I didn't want to interfere because we all went through it at some point in our young lives, and I wanted you to learn from the experience. But a mother's instinct is always right."

Then she continued, "I knew it was Chris. He is a nice boy and comes from a decent family. I know his mother well, and he always calls here looking for you, so I knew it was him."

Crystal said, "No, mother, it is not Chris. He is someone else. You don't know him."

Dorothy said, "Is he an older guy? I know you are very stubborn and picky."

"No, mother. He is in my class. His name is Manny."

"That's an unusual name. I never heard of it."

"He is from India and wears a turban."

Dorothy felt a lump in her throat and took a deep breath. She was silent, shocked that Crystal was dating a brown guy. She didn't know what to say. Dorothy told her daughters that they could date anyone they wanted as long as they were happy. But she never had thought in a million years that her older daughter, Crystal, would date someone from a different race. She didn't want to break her daughter's heart, so she pretended to accept Manny.

Crystal said, "I have invited him over next week for Thanksgiving Day, so you and Dad can meet him. We will all have dinner together."

Dorothy looked at Crystal and said, "I will tell your father, but don't move too fast with this relationship, okay?"

Crystal replied, "We have been dating for over a year. I really love him."

Dorothy was speechless and couldn't believe what she was hearing. She still couldn't come to terms with this new information that her daughter trusted her with and thought maybe it was a dream that Crystal was going out with a brown guy whom she never had any intention of meeting or introducing to her husband. She knew he would hate the idea of Crystal being with someone who was brown and wore a turban. But after her daughter pleaded for them to meet him, she decided to give young Manny a chance because she trusted her daughter's instincts and knew she had good judgement. In the back of her mind, she was also curious to see how this young boy was, if he was any good or whether he was disrespectful. But her father's reaction might be another story. He would never be okay with Manny being brown.

Dorothy waited till Crystal's dad, Tom, came back from work.

She said, "Hi honey, I have something really important to discuss with you."

Tom said, "Ok, dear! What is it? Fire away."

Dorothy said, "Sit down. Look, I don't want you to get upset, okay?"

Tom said, "Oookaayyy!"

"Crystal has a boyfriend, and she is bringing him to Thanksgiving dinner."

Tom looked at her and said, "Ohhh, ok, no problem. Is it that boy, Chris?"

"Umm . . . no, it is someone else."

"Okay," said Tom, "No big deal. It's puppy love. Who is it?"

"It is a boy from India. His name is Manny, and he wears a turban."

Tom became angry and said, "Are you fucking kidding me? This is a joke, right? There is no way in hell my daughter is dating a fucking brown piece of shit, no fucking way possible. Is it a prank? Please tell me it's a prank. I am going to puke. Fucking gross! I am going to have a word with Crystal right now and tell her to break it off. He will not be allowed here. I can't believe that she won't go out with anybody white at least."

"You are not going to say anything to her. She did nothing wrong. We both trust our daughter, don't we?"

Tom stormed out, saying, "Fucking unbelievable!" and took off in his car.

Crystal overheard everything and started to cry in her room.

Her mother went in and said, "Honey, your father is being overprotective of you, that's all."

Crystal looked at her mother with tears rolling down her cheeks and said, "I love Manny. It doesn't matter to me if he wears a turban or is brown, black, yellow, or white. I look at him as a human. My soul connects with his soul through the stars. I can't explain it, mother. I can't explain it. I think about him all day and all night."

Dorothy gave Crystal a big hug, wiped her tears, and said, "All I want is for you to be happy. I love you."

The next day, Dorothy made Tom understand that they should at least give Manny a chance, even if they disapproved of the relationship.

"We raised our daughter right and have always told her that she can date anyone she wants. We just want her to be happy but her dating a Muslim or a brown person with a turban, no way! I was really shocked to hear the news as well and couldn't believe that she was in a relationship with a brown guy, but look at our beautiful daughter's face. It lights up when she talks about Manny. It means she really does care for him, and he means a lot to her. So, I guess, let's give him a chance. I would like to get to know the boy and what kind of person he is at least."

Tom grunted and said, "You are wrong. I don't have to like him. I guess she does, but I can't process it. I'll have a word with her, anyway. Let's hope it's just a phase she is going through."

Tom still couldn't believe that Crystal had started dating this brown kid. Knowing how beautiful and smart she was, she could have had anybody she wanted but had to pick the brown boy.

It was Thanksgiving Day, and Manny dressed up to go to Crystal's house. He was somewhat nervous about meeting her parents for the very first time but knew he had to do so for Crystal. Manny rang the doorbell. Crystal rushed downstairs with her little sister and opened the door. Manny was standing there with flowers and a box of chocolates.

Crystal said, "Thanks, honey! This is my younger sister, Tiffany."

Manny smiled and said hello to her little sister, and then Crystal asked Manny to come in the house and sit down on the couch.

She smiled and said, "My parents will be coming soon."

Dorothy walked into the room, a little nervous.

She waved a little with her fingers and said, "Hi, you must be Manny. I'm Crystal's mother, Dorothy."

Manny offered Dorothy his hand, but Dorothy quickly turned around.

As she was leaving the room, Manny said, "Please wait, I have something for you and your family."

Dorothy, a bit uneasy, stopped and turned around, wondering what Manny wanted.

He handed her a box of chocolates and said, "This is for you. I'm Manny," with a big smile.

Dorothy thought, "Hmm, he is polite and brought us a present."

She said, "Thank you! Dinner will be served soon. Crystal, your father should be here any minute."

Just as she said that Tom walked into the room and didn't look at Manny. Manny said hello and offered Tom his hand. But Tom just walked right past him into the kitchen.

Dorothy was busy in the kitchen.

A few minutes later, she said, "Dinner is served."

All of them got off the couch, and Crystal apologized to Manny, "My father is acting that way because I am the oldest daughter and the first one to date in the family. Don't take it personally."

Manny felt unwanted, very hurt by the way Tom had acted towards him. Manny had felt this tension from elementary school through to high school. He felt he was treated as if he didn't belong and was not accepted because of his skin colour and turban, like he was an alien from another planet. But he kept his feelings inside and went along with what Crystal said because he loved her and would do anything for her. As they proceeded to the dinner table, Manny felt uneasiness, nervousness, dislike, and anxiety brewing between himself and Crystal's parents, especially Tom.

When everyone finally sat down at the dinner table, before anyone could start eating, Tom said grace: "Thank you, God, for this food and those who prepared it, in Jesus' name. Amen."

This was all new to Manny. He didn't know when to say amen. He felt embarrassed for his ignorance and apologized, but Tom locked his angry eyes with Manny's terrified eyes with a menacing stare that his daughters or his wife had never seen. For 30 seconds, everyone around the table froze. Then, they began to eat. Manny felt uncomfortable at the table and helped himself to two slices of turkey and no sides. Crystal was shocked because Manny always had a big appetite. She told him not to be shy.

Then Dorothy said, "Look Manny, please eat more. We made a lot of food."

Manny's taste buds activated, and he began to serve himself mashed potatoes, steamed carrots, corn on the cob, and a big turkey leg, which he poured gravy over. He was feeling out of place and didn't want anyone to see how much he could eat, so he didn't have seconds.

Crystal said, "Manny, you have a big appetite, but you didn't even eat any pumpkin pie."

Even though he felt like eating the pie, Manny was very shy and didn't want Crystal's parents to feel they had to sit with him as he ate.

Manny got up and said, "Thank you, Dorothy! The food was excellent, I appreciate you all having me here. I have never had this kind of dinner in my life; I had never tried turkey or gravy," and he looked at Tom and thanked him as well.

Dorothy said, "You're welcome!"

Tom didn't care that Manny was polite and awkward.

Then, Tiffany, who was about four years younger than Crystal, asked Manny, "What is that on top of your head?"

Crystal said "Shhhhhhhhhh, Tiffany!"

Manny looked at Tiffany and said, "It's okay. Everyone is wondering here, so I will go ahead and tell you the short version. It is a part of my religious background. The turban is sacred, and it was worn for protection when the *Gurkhas* were fighting against the Mongols in India about 500 years ago, and also when they fought with the British army to defeat Hitler. It protects our heads. We are equipped with five Ks: *kesh* (uncut hair), *kara* (steel bracelet), *kangha* (wooden comb), *kachchha* (cotton underwear), and *kirpan* (steel sword). We believe every religion and race are equal. Our religion helps everyone. We feed people at our temples. We call it *langar*. It provides free food to anybody regardless of their religion or background.

Dorothy, Crystal, and Tiffany were listening and were amazed at what it meant to be Sikh. They learned something new and found it very interesting, but Tom didn't care about it.

He thought, "My daughter is dating a Muslim."

After everyone had eaten dessert, except Manny, Crystal said to him, "Let's watch a movie downstairs."

Manny agreed and thanked Dorothy and Tom once again for inviting him.

The lovebirds went downstairs, and Dorothy sent Tiffany to wash up before bed. She and Tom began washing the dishes.

Dorothy whispered to Tom, "So what do you think of Manny?"

"I'm sorry, Dorothy, I don't like him. I don't trust him or his religious way. I feel like he is just gonna use and hurt our daughter and then go marry his own kind. In his religion, they beat their wives all the time and treat them like shit. I don't think I will be speaking to him anymore. If she wants to date him, well I can't stop her. She is growing up, and even if I try to stop her, I'm pretty sure she will see him behind my back. So, I'm staying out of it and seeing how it all goes from here. I am not interested in what he likes or anything or what he wants to do when he gets out of high school. I just want to protect my daughter, and if he ever hurts her, I'll have his head."

"Oh Tom," Dorothy said, "I think he is a bright, respectable young man. He is polite, well mannered, and good looking. I can see what Crystal sees in him. He is shy and sweet."

Tom looked at Dorothy and whispered, "You're falling into his trap too. Don't you see he is a brown Hindu or Muslim or whatever he is? He is just pretending to be nice. Remember that these people have no respect for their women. He ate like a pig and made a big mess and didn't show any manners. The freak didn't even know when to say amen. That tells me a lot! So, I'm just saying that if he ever hurts my daughter, I will cut off his fucking brown balls along with the diaper on his head. I don't feel good. My stomach feels upset. I'm going to bed, and please, no more talking about little Gandhi."

Dorothy said, "You always said you won't mind who our daughters date. Do you have a problem just because this young man is not white? You seemed to change your liberal attitude very fast."

Dorothy quietly finished washing the dishes, while Tom went into the living room and turned on the television.

After a couple of hours, the lovebirds had finished watching their movie, and Crystal was going to bed. Before Manny left, he gave Crystal a big kiss on the lips and a big hug. He told her that he loved her. He got back home and quietly snuck in through the window he left half-open, so nobody would notice when he came in.

Christmas would be coming soon, and Manny was no longer a stranger to the Kleen household. He was at Crystal's house practically every day. He brought presents for everyone, and on Christmas Day, they would have a big turkey and eat a big dessert.

After a while, Tom started ignoring Manny, but Dorothy liked Manny, so she would always greet him. Manny was starting to grow very close to the family. He would mow their lawn, babysit, and often help Dorothy unload the groceries from her car. Tom didn't appreciate anything Manny did in his yard. He told Manny that he had ruined his grass by cutting it and to never touch his lawnmower again. He would cut it himself on the weekends. Manny looked at Tom, apologized, and said that he would never do it again and that he just wanted to help Tom because he was working so much and Dorothy had asked him to.

Tom told Dorothy, "Look, I can do my own yard work around here, okay? I don't need anybody's help. If I do, I'll ask for it."

Manny was sad at times, thinking if his skin were white, he wouldn't be treated this way. All he wanted was for Tom to accept him for who he was. Although he never expressed it to Crystal, he was very hurt.

CHAPTER 15

On the last Friday of every month, Tom would go for drinks at the local tavern and meet his friends for a guys' night out. They would have a few beers, play pool and keno, eat wings, and maybe watch the game. They were all talking about their children and wives or girlfriends. After a few drinks, Tom said to the guys that his fucking daughter was going out with a turban bastard, a brown piece of shit, and he didn't like it. He told everyone how he cut his lawn wrong and always wanted to help him. He started laughing out of anger.

One of his friends was Jack, who used to work with Mr. Singh at the mill.

He said, "I wonder if it's his boy or not. It doesn't matter; all of them fucking Hindus are the same. His father or uncle swung a knife at me because the guys poured ketchup on his turban. Be careful of these Muslims. Mr. Singh was an idiot. He worked through his shifts and stank like curry, and he had a Barbie lunch box. Hahahaha!"

Tom started laughing too.

Jack said, "Hey, I have an idea. If that brown boy wants to help you so bad, let's get him to my friend Ken. He has a construction company, and his employees never show up on the weekend. How about you get the brown kid to give me a call, and let's see if he can do a man's work or not? Maybe he won't be able to handle it, and your daughter will see what a pussy he is. Hahahaha!"

After a few more beers and chicken wings, Tom said, "You know what? Why not? I want to see if he is for real or not. If he's a wimp, it's a great way to show it!"

Jack said, "No problem, have him ready by 7 a.m. on Saturday at your place. Ken's son will pick him up. I promise I will take care of him really good; leave him with me."

The next day, Tom said to Dorothy, "Can you let Manny know that I need his help next Saturday? My friend needs a hand."

Dorothy said, "Wow, what has changed? You've had a change of heart. That's nice, Tom! Why don't you ask him yourself? He would really like that. Maybe you guys can get over the hump and start to communicate with each other. Crystal would love for you guys to talk too."

"No, no, let's take it slow. Get Manny to come here Saturday at 7 a.m."

Dorothy asked Crystal to tell Manny that her father wanted him to help him out on Saturday.

Crystal smiled, hugged her dad, and said, "Thank you, Dad, for letting Manny finally help you."

Tom said, "Hold on, princess! We need to take it slow here. He will be helping my friend this Saturday. Then we will see."

Manny was excited that Crystal's father had accepted him in a small way. He assured Crystal that he would not let her father down. Excited all week, Manny told his parents that he was going to work at the school on Saturday. They had a job for him. Mr. Singh was happy with the idea of him working. Manjot also insisted that it was good for him to learn something. So, Mr.

Singh thought it was a good idea to stay out of Manny's way to let him work out the details on his own.

On Friday night, Manjot packed lunch for Manny because he was going to work the next morning. He walked up to Crystal's house at five minutes to seven and knocked on her door. She opened the door and gave Manny a big kiss with a smile.

She said, "Have fun at work. I made an extra-special lunch just in case you work late. I made you heart-shaped cookies with stars on them and a peanut butter and jelly sandwich. Thank you so much! It really means a lot to me to see you and my dad finally getting along."

Manny smiled and said, "Same here. I'm glad I could help your father too. I love you, my shining star."

Ken's construction truck pulled up, and he honked the horn.

Manny ran up to the front door of the truck, opened the door, and said, "Hi, my name is Manny," with his hand extended.

Ken's son, Jim, who was driving the truck, said, "Get in the back!" without even saying hello. He drove straight to the work site.

Jim, the work site manager, was a few years older than Manny. Jack and Ken were there too. Jack observed Manny getting out of the truck and said to Ken, "Yup, that's the Hindu's son at the mill. He looks like him."

Jack said, "Let me tell him what to do."

Manny politely introduced himself to Jack, extended his hand, and asked where he could put his lunch bag.

Jack said rudely, "No time for talking. You were late today. Leave your bag in the truck and come over here now!"

Manny, a bit startled, listened to Jack. He gave Manny the shovel and told him to dig and not stop unless he said so. Ken and Jim observed from 10 feet away and saw Jack commanding

Manny, telling him to hurry and pointing and yelling at Manny. A few hours had gone by, and Manny was working hard, shovelling, filling up the wheelbarrow, and dumping the dirt to the other side. Ken told Jim to give Manny a half-hour break because the young lad had been working hard, and Jim agreed.

After Ken left, Jack went up to Jim and said, "If we don't deteriorate them now, more of them will come to Canada to take our jobs. So, Jim, let's go in the truck and let him work."

After some time, it started to rain very hard, and Manny was still shovelling while it was pouring. Manny's turban and clothes got all wet. He looked back at the truck, the lights went on, and Jim and Jack took off, leaving Manny stranded in the rain. Jack asked Jim to pull over.

Jack said, "Let's see, what have we got in his lunch? Haha!"

Jim said, "Are you sure it's okay to go through his lunch? My father told me to give him a break. I know you have to be tough on the workers, but it is pouring rain, and he has not eaten or drunk anything for five hours. He has been working all this time."

Jack said, "Like I said, I don't want his people in my country. Let's see what's in his bag."

They saw heart-shaped cookies and a peanut butter and jelly sandwich. Jack finished all the cookies and drinks and told Jim to go back to the workplace. Manny was standing there, shivering in the rain.

Jack got out of the truck and said, "Did I tell you to stop? Turn around and work!"

Manny turned around.

Jack told Jim, "You're his age. Hit him in the leg with a shovel."

Jim looked at Jack as if he were crazy.

"I don't know. I don't think my father will approve."

"Do it! DO IT! Now!"

Jim grabbed a shovel and went behind Manny but then went back to the truck and said to Jack, "This is not right."

Jack came out of the truck and pushed Manny into the mud.

Jim couldn't believe what Jack did and ran up to Manny and said, "Oh, Manny! Are you ok?" Manny looked at him with an angry face. Jim apologized to Manny and told him he had no idea Jack was going to do that.

Jack decided it was time for him to leave, so he got in his truck and took off. Jim pulled Manny up, and Manny started shovelling again, thinking about Crystal.

He thought "I'm not going to wimp out. I'm determined to show her father that I'm worthy of her love."

Jim said, "Let's stop working. You worked hard enough, and you're soaking wet. Let's go home."

On the way, he gave Manny a chocolate bar and a pop and said he felt terrible about what Jack did to him.

Tom, through the window, observed Manny soaked and covered in mud, thinking, "Wow, he does work hard. I'm surprised he lasted."

Crystal brought Manny in, dried him off, and gave him some warm soup. Then, she asked Manny if he had a good day at work. He nodded unsmilingly but didn't want to let Crystal know how he truly felt. He just wanted her father to accept him.

Jack phoned Tom and said, "I need Manny again for Ken," and Tom agreed.

He told Crystal to have Manny at their house by 7 a.m. the following Saturday. Manny didn't look too enthusiastic when Crystal asked him to work again. He was having a hard time sleeping because he kept remembering Jack yelling at him.

When Saturday arrived, Manny was anxious but still arrived at Crystal's door at the agreed-upon time. He refused the lunch

Crystal gave him and left without giving her a kiss. She knew something wasn't right.

Jack was honking the horn and said, "Why are you always fucking late, Manny?"

Manny looked at him and kept quiet. He sat in the back of the truck and asked if Ken and Jim were not coming.

"I said I would work with you, and another big, strong boy will be helping us. So, shut the hell up and fucking work hard. I don't want you to talk. Just work."

Luckily for Manny, the weather was at least nice.

Jack dropped off Manny with a shovel, threw his lunch in the puddle, and said, "Next time, don't leave it in the fucking truck, dipshit."

Jack picked up two boys to work with Manny and explained to them that Jim and Ken were not there and that he was in charge. He explained to the boys that he wanted the other boy who was working there to feel like he never wanted to come back again, and at the end of the day they were going to beat up the boy, and Jack was going to pay them.

One of the boys started helping Manny shovel. The other boy stayed with Jack. He was going to unload concrete because he was bigger and stronger. The boy working with Manny was named Kevin. After an hour, he crossed-checked Manny in the back with the shovel. Manny got up and asked him why he did that. Then he pushed and crossed-checked Kevin. Jack liked what he saw. He told the other boy to help Kevin. When Kevin saw his big friend coming, he grabbed a rock and threw it at Manny. Then, Kevin grabbed Manny's turban. Manny grabbed Kevin's hands. Then, Kevin's big friend pushed Kevin to the ground. Kevin and Jack were startled to see what was happening. Kevin couldn't believe it. He got up and ran back to where Jack was. They were both observing what the big guy was going to do.

Manny looked at this other big boy, surprised by his actions until he saw his face. "Lee!"

Lee said, "Manny, wow, it's been a long time."

They gave each other a big hug. Kevin and Jack couldn't believe it.

"You don't live at your old place anymore, and I never see you at school. You have grown."

"Yes, Manny, my friend. We had to move to the neighbouring small town. I haven't been in touch with anybody. Lately, I saw Ravy hanging out with some people in my town. As for Jason, I haven't seen him since elementary school."

"Yes, Jason moved away. I'm glad you are doing better these days."

Lee smiled and said, "I miss your mother's roti at your house and all the Twinkies and Ding Dongs you used to give me. I will never forget your mother giving me clothes and lunch. You were a very good friend, and I will always be by your side."

Jack was furious to see what happened.

He went up to Lee and said, "Get him!"

Lee grabbed the shovel, "Get who? You? You fucking asshole."

Lee ran after Jack with the shovel, telling Manny to get out of there while he did, and said that he would be in touch with him.

Later, Lee called the owner of the company to explain what had happened, and Jim confirmed Lee's allegations. Jack was never allowed to work with them again. Ken told Tom the story. Tom felt bad for Manny because, after the incident, he had walked all the way back home. It took him two hours. Tom hadn't realized what Jack had done to Manny. It wasn't a nice thing to do. Crystal told Manny never to work with her father again and was disappointed with her father. Manny agreed there was no need for him to impress anyone. He told his shining star he loved her and kissed her.

Weeks later, when Manny was visiting, Dorothy asked him, "What do you want to be when you grow up?"

Manny said, "I love working on cars. I want to be a mechanic. My neighbour taught me when I was young, and I fell in love with it."

"That's nice. Tom is a plumber by trade, and I work in an accounting office," replied Dorothy. Then she asked, "What do your parents do?"

Manny felt a little anxious. He didn't answer the question and left the room.

Dorothy would always ask Crystal why she had never gone over to Manny's place to meet his parents. Crystal would make up excuses and change the subject. Crystal and Manny would get into arguments about it as well because he kept telling her that he would take her home to meet his parents one day, but he always kept making excuses.

Three years had passed, and it was a cold, rainy day in November. Manny was walking across to John's house and noticed him outside with his cane and cigar. He was just sitting there. He walked over and asked John if he needed a hand getting into the house, helped him into the garage so he didn't get wet, and sat him down in his chair. His cane was left outside, so Manny went and grabbed it.

John said to Manny, "You are so grown up. You used to come over every day when you were a little boy and pet Toby, and I showed you how to fix cars, fly a kite, and even helped you get on your bike when you fell off. How you used to ride your bike to and from school. I know you're all grown up. Do you have a girlfriend?" John started smiling, "I see you sneaking out at night."

Manny said, "Father John, yes I do. You're the only one who knows. I haven't even told my parents yet. They will kill me! I would love to bring her over and for them to meet her. I love her so much! I dream about her and think about her all day and all night. What should I do?"

"My son, I love you like my very own son that I never had. So, I'm going to tell you that one important thing in life is to go with your heart. Your family will understand. Never give up. Remember when you fell off your bike when you were young and started to cry and didn't want to ride it anymore? What did I tell you that time?"

"You said I had the heart of a lion. So, I should roar and get back on my bike and ride it. No matter how much I hurt, the pain will go away!"

"Yes, my son! Always remember that in life, okay?"

Manny hugged John and said, "I love you."

John said, "I love you too. This is the year you are going to graduate. Treat your girlfriend like gold and get her to come over to meet your parents. Tell her how much you love her, and I will always be on your side. Bertha and I would love to meet her one day as well. We are going to come to your graduation, even if we can't move that well. We love you, and you are in our hearts forever, my son."

Manny felt good every time he talked to John. He was like the father he never had. He felt he could tell him anything. He respected and loved him, even though he didn't go over to his house as much as he used to.

Manny went home to bed. Manjot was working full-time at night cleaning houses, and Mr. Singh was still plugging away at the mill. This was Manny's year to graduate from high school. By now, he had gotten his driver's licence and his own Mazda. His relationship with Crystal was still strong, and they were planning to get married in a few years. Ravy would be the best man, and Tina would be the maid of honour.

CHAPTER 16

The next day, Manny woke up early to the sound of sirens. Mr. Singh had gone to work, and Manjot was sleeping after doing the night shift. He noticed ambulances and police cars in front of John's house. He threw on his pants and rushed over to their house. He saw Bertha hunched over and crying out loud. Manny put his arms around Bertha and asked her what happened.

"John passed away last night in his sleep."

Manny started wailing loudly, "Nooooo! Nooooo! Nooooo!"

After 20 minutes of him sobbing, Manjot woke up and came running over to find out what had happened. She started crying when she found out. They were all mourning John's death. Manny did not go to school that day, and he and Manjot stayed at the Smith's house all day, helping Bertha. Then, later that evening, Manny visited Crystal and told her everything. She supported him and hugged him. She told him that she was there for him if he needed anything and understood if he had to help his old neighbour.

The next day, both of John's daughters and other relatives came over to the house to support Bertha. Manny missed school again and stayed at his house. His mother took a few days off work as well. Mr. Singh felt a little compassion for John. He knew he was a good man and helped his family whenever they needed it, and he was good to his son too. He did have a small tear in his eye for John, even though in front of his family he acted as if he didn't care for the old man. Mr. Singh told Manjot they were going to donate something to Bertha and that he was also going to John's funeral on Saturday. Manny was pleased that his father was going to go to the funeral instead of going to work. He was happy that his father was showing signs of being an emotional person and not a robot who only toiled.

Many people attended the funeral, especially John's family from out of town and customers he had served who knew John as a mechanic. Manny made a speech at the funeral, recalling how he met John and all the fun things they had done together—how he taught him to ride his bike and fly a kite—and how he inspired him to become a mechanic. Then, out of the corner of his eye, he saw Tom, Dorothy, and Crystal.

Then he paused and ended the eulogy with a tear in his eye by saying, "This is what John would say to me. These were his words when I first fell off my bike. I was around six years old, and I didn't want to ride it anymore. I hated the bike, and I wished I never had it. Then John came over and said life has its ups and downs. You're gonna feel pain and sadness, but you have to get up and get on the bike and start riding it because *you have the heart of a lion. Let's hear you roar. Never give up!* So, I got back up, even though I didn't want to. I felt so much pain in my knees because they were cut up and my arms were scratched, but I just got on my bike and started to ride, and the pain and my tears went away. After all, John was right. When you fall down, you have to get up and get on your feet again, and that lesson he taught me will stay with me forever. I will never forget that he made me the man I am today. I will always love him as a second father and Bertha as a second mother. Rest in peace, John. I love you, and God bless you and your family."

As Manny went outside the funeral hall to catch his breath from all the tears and emotions he was feeling from his speech, Crystal noticed him going out. She approached him and hugged him. Manny put his head on Crystal's shoulder and began to cry. She put her hand on his cheeks, and she gently wiped off the tears that flowed from Manny's eyes with her fingertips. She gripped him tightly.

Mr. Singh went outside to tell Manny something and saw Crystal and Manny hugging each other. Mr. Singh froze, and Manjot came outside as well. She was also shocked when she saw them. She whispered to Mr. Singh to come back inside, but he didn't want to leave. Then they went back inside without Manny noticing. Mr. Singh was observing Manny from far away to see what he was doing. Then he saw Crystal's mom come and hug Manny, and Crystal's father was in the background. He was interested in what his son was doing with this Caucasian family and how he was interacting with them. Jarnal was right. He had explained to Mr. Singh why Manny was never home and his attitude had changed. He was becoming a grown-up young man. Mr. Singh was terrified of what he saw.

Manjot walked over to Mr. Singh and told him, "Let's go home. This is not the place to start a fight with our son. He is grown up. He can make his own decisions."

Mr. Singh said, "You're right. He is too old to be told what to do, and I am also growing old. He is not a kid anymore. He is experiencing being a teenager, so that's why I slapped him that day he went to the dance. I already knew he had a girlfriend. I didn't tell you, but I will make him a man and give him responsibilities like a man now. This is actually good. Jarnal told me already about his little girlfriend long before. We have a plan. Jarnal is a very smart, far-sighted man. He told me not to be mad about it, and I'm not. We have an excellent plan for our entire family once he is done high school. After he finishes high school, we will move to Toronto. It is a big city; there are more of our people there and more opportunities for work. It will be a better place for our son to raise his new family once he is married. I haven't been going to Toronto for the past 10 years for two weeks every summer for nothing, dear. We have a beautiful house that I purchased there. It's outside of Toronto and is close to my cousin's house. Jarnal's sister lives out there, and they have been showing me pictures of this young, beautiful Indian girl who is going to get her Visa and is coming to Toronto next year. She comes from a good Indian family and is pursuing a doctorate. She is very nice. Jarnal has been telling me about her for a year now to get Manny to meet her and get married to this nice Indian girl. I am so excited about this. I worked my whole life for this, dear. Finally, our dream will come true."

Manjot said, "What about Manny? He has made so many friends here, and we have our home here."

Mr. Singh said, "Manjot, think about this. We are living in a small town. There is nothing in store for the future of our son and our future grandkids, so why not take advantage of this opportunity. I have a job already set up at a steel factory in Toronto. My cousin is the president of this company. Manny can work there too, and the pay is really good. My cousin said that in six months, he will promote me to a managerial position so I won't have to do hard labour. There are better schools, shops, restaurants, and more of our people. There is a *Gurudwara* nearby. Just you and I will go in a couple of months for a few weeks, and you can see for yourself how it is. We will still keep our house here and rent it out. When Manny graduates, we will move in the summer, okay? Let him finish high school and graduate. We don't want to bother him too much. I will not fight with him or be mad at anything because we are so close to the best days of our lives. We will invite all our families to the reception and wedding. It will be beautiful. I can't wait for the day. This is my plan. Trust me, we both want what's the best for our son, and him hanging out with his white girlfriend will soon be over once we leave this place. I don't want him to be hurt by white girls because one minute they are with someone, and the next minute, they are with someone new."

Manjot was ambivalent. She didn't want to see her little Manny hurt. She knew this decision wasn't going to be easy because she always said she wanted the best for her son, and nothing would stand in his way.

Manjot told Kuljit about their plan to move to Toronto once Manny graduated and told her not to tell anyone. She asked Kuljit if Ravy ever mentioned to her that Manny might have a girlfriend or not.

Kuljit laughed, "I wouldn't worry about it, my sister. They are young men now. Of course, they are gonna have girlfriends. Don't be silly. Anyway, let's change the topic."

Kuljit said that she had been to Toronto once when she first came to Canada and stayed there for six months before coming out west. She described how big and beautiful the city was and how much there was to do. All the people from India and all the Indian shops and restaurants made it feel like little India. She wished that she would have stayed there. Manjot was excited to go and couldn't wait to see it for herself.

Mr. Singh had already made all the arrangements. He and Jarnal agreed that his last day at the sawmill would be July 1st, after Manny graduated.

The next day at school, Crystal was with Manny at lunch and said, "Were they your parents at the funeral standing with you?"

Manny replied, "Yes, they were."

Crystal said, "Wow, your father is big and was wearing a nice yellow turban, and your mother had a beautiful Indian suit on. I wish I could have met them."

"Yes, you will, I promise. But you will do so once we graduate because they both have a rule about not dating until I am older. So, for now, let's keep it this way. Okay, my love? I love you."

Manny knew his father would never accept Crystal until he could move out and wasn't sure about what his mother's attitude would be but thought if he told them how he really felt, maybe they would accept her.

Spring break arrived fast, and Manny was surprised that both of his parents were going away for two weeks. They had never gone on vacation together ever in their life, and he was surprised they were going to leave him all by himself. He noticed his dad was suddenly laid back and was being extra nice to him.

Mr. Singh said, "Manny!"

"Yes, Papa."

"Your mother and I are going to Toronto for a couple of weeks, okay? Here are the keys to my van if you need them. Your mother filled up on groceries already, and I have left you money for whenever you need it. Oh, and Aunty Kuljit will be checking up on you, and you can call her or even Uncle Jarnal if you need anything. I have also bought Rocky dog food. If you want to keep him inside downstairs at night, go right ahead."

Manny was so excited about being left alone, the first day they left for Toronto, he threw a party. Ravy, Crystal, and Tina, all came to Manny's house. Jass got them alcohol. A few other classmates came over too. They partied all night, and the next day

Crystal was in bed with Manny. All day, they made love to each other and had breakfast and dinner in bed. Ravy was often there with Tina. They were sharing the bed downstairs, their romance having been rekindled.

The news about the parties at Manny's house started spreading through the grapevine. More and more of his schoolmates showed up, and they were partying every day. Crystal wasn't going home all this time, and then later in the week, Tom pulled up to Manny's house and started knocking on his door.

Manny opened the door with his shirt off, and Tom said, "Where the heck is my daughter?"

He walked into Manny's house, saw all the booze, grabbed Crystal by the arm, and took her home.

On the way out, he said, "I will be talking to your parents, young man, and Crystal is grounded for a month!"

Tom took Crystal home. She was a little tipsy and smelled like booze. Dorothy wasn't impressed with her daughter's behaviour, and they both agreed that she had to be grounded for two weeks and Tom would have a word with Manny's parents.

Three days before Manny's parents were going to return home, the house was a mess. So, Manny had Ravy help him clean up everything. Later that day, Kuljit showed up out of the blue and walked right into the house. She went into the backyard and caught Ravy and Manny smoking with their shirts off.

Kuljit said, "Boys, it looks like you guys were having crazy fun?"

The boys both got up and were shocked that Ravy's mother was standing there. They quickly put out the cigarettes and tried to explain that they were someone else's and that they were just trying it. Kuljit was unconcerned.

She said, "Okay, boys, let's clean up the house before Manny's parents come back."

Manny was still in shock and said, "Yes, Aunty."

She didn't say anything about them smoking, so the boys started to clean the house, and Kuljit gave them a hand.

Manny asked Ravy, worried, "Do you think your mom's gonna tell my mom?"

Kuljit overheard and responded, "I am not going to tell your parents, so don't worry about it. My husband smokes and drinks all the time."

Manny sighed with relief.

The Singhs finally came back from their vacation in Toronto, and the house was immaculate, cleaner than when they had left it.

Spring break was over, and the kids went back to school. Manjot couldn't believe how nice the big city was. She called over Kuljit to share everything. Manjot was so happy. She and Mr. Singh went out for dinner, went sightseeing, visited relatives, and she got to see their new home. She told Kuljit how big the house was, and that it was near the city, and everything was close by, even the *Gurudwara*. She told Kuljit that she was in love with the city and wanted to move there and how her relationship with Mr. Singh had changed for the better. She also talked about how beautiful the girl who was coming from India was. She told Kuljit that her name was Sonjot, and she was pursuing her bachelor's degree in India. Manjot also shared that she was planning to get Manny married to her as soon as she moved to Toronto next year and that all the family was excited for Manny. Mr. Singh already had the reception hall and *Gurudwara* booked for the wedding next year and told all his relatives. They had printed the wedding invitation cards, and Mr. Singh was bragging to all his relatives that he would host the biggest wedding by far and his son had graduated and would become a mechanic.

Manjot continued, "Don't worry, *saheli*! You guys are invited too. Maybe I should find you a girl for Ravy as well."

Kuljit laughed, "I don't think my son wants to get married just yet, and I think he wants to marry his own girlfriend. I was gonna ask if you were totally sure about Manny being married because he has a girlfriend and the same with Ravy. He is still very young to get married at this point. Don't you think you guys are rushing him? And I don't mind who Ravy marries. I never want to force him to get married."

CHAPTER 17

Manjot felt she wasn't being fair to her son and his wishes but told Kuljit that Mr. Singh was older now, and he just wanted to make sure his son was set for a good life before something happened to him.

Manjot wondered if she was being brainwashed by Mr. Singh since he kept saying, "You want your kids to have a good life by marrying an Indian girl. White girls don't stay. They are with someone one day and another guy another day, and they divorce fast."

Manjot was conflicted and thought maybe Manny's girlfriend was a kind, good-hearted young lady and decided not to judge her. She never gave her little boy a chance to bring his girlfriend over to introduce her to them. She felt slightly guilty about it.

Kuljit smiled and said, "You have to be careful about your decision. This is Canada and not India. You said you always wanted to see your boy happy, and so you really have to go with your gut. If he really loves this girl, let them be. By the way, I would never pressure my son into marrying against his will. I wish you and your family good luck when you guys leave."

Manjot sat there not knowing what to do. She thought maybe it would be for the best if Manny married his own kind. It was not normal to have an interracial wedding. She feared everyone in the Indian community gossiping about Manny marrying a Caucasian lady and that he would be considered an outcast because he didn't marry within his own community. Mr. Singh's name and family reputation would be diminished, and he would be upset and angry.

Crystal had only a few days left of being grounded. Manny and Crystal were still seeing each other at school but weren't allowed to see each other otherwise till her punishment was over. So, at school, they tried to spend every second they could together.

Later that evening when Manny was at home, Manjot was at work, and Mr. Singh had just come back from the mill, Manny heard a knock on the front door. He opened the door and saw Tom.

Tom said, "Can I speak to your father?"

Manny was so nervous he didn't know what to do. This couldn't possibly end well! Mr. Singh was right behind Manny. He told Manny to get out of the way.

Tom saw this hulking Indian man with a yellow turban and long beard standing in front of him. It made Tom nervous, and he said, "Singh? Are you Mr. Singh?"

Mr. Singh said, "Yes, I am. How can I help you?"

Tom explained in detail everything that had happened at home while the Singhs went on vacation—how Manny was partying with his daughter and how so many girls and boys were getting drunk. How could he leave his 18-year-old boy alone at home? Mr. Singh wrote down Tom's phone number and address and assured Tom that Manny would be disciplined. What happened was not acceptable. Tom felt confident and relieved that Mr. Singh was going to straighten Manny out. He looked very religious, and maybe that would discourage Manny from seeing his daughter.

Manny ran into his room, his anxiety rising. He anticipated a beating.

Then Mr. Singh gently opened the door to his bedroom and said, "Son, sit down."

Manny looked at him, surprised.

Mr. Singh said, "We all have to go to Toronto. Your uncle is sick. When you graduate, me, you, and your mother will need to visit him."

Manny quickly agreed and asked if they would be away for only a couple of weeks. Mr. Singh said yes.

Manny agreed so he could get out of trouble. His dad was talking to him so gently. He had never seen this side of him before. Manny felt loved by his father for the first time in his life. Mr. Singh gave Manny a big hug and told him he loved him and had worked hard for him all his life and was willing to give him anything he wanted. It felt good finally being accepted by his father. He thought that it might be a good time to tell him about his relationship with his girlfriend because he noticed a change in his father, and perhaps he would be willing to accept Crystal. But Manny was still puzzled about how his father was acting, especially after he had thrown a big party with white girls and the boys.

In the coming weeks, Manny was having the best time of his life. His father said that he didn't have a curfew anymore, and he was allowed to go out whenever he wanted. His mother couldn't believe how her husband was treating her. He had become respectful and cared about her needs. He had always been there financially but never emotionally. She wondered why he hadn't been like this when Manny was young and when she wanted to explore and experience life but found it difficult. Manjot and Manny didn't complain about Mr. Singh's past behaviour anymore. They went with the flow and liked the new Mr. Singh. Manny and Manjot had all the freedom they wanted and took advantage of it. He even sneaked in Crystal at home through the window at night without his parents knowing anything.

In June, Manny and Crystal graduated, and they were both going to the prom in a week.

Manny approached his mother after school when both of them were home alone and said, "mom, I have to talk to you. It is very important."

Manjot looked at her son and said, "Okay, my beautiful boy. What do you want to say?"

Manny said, "mom, all of this time in high school, I had a girlfriend. Her name is Crystal. I really love her a lot. I think about her all the time and can't get over her. I want you and Papa to meet her. She is the love of my life, and I want to be with her for the rest of my life."

Manjot felt the love from her little boy's heart to hers. She could see the love he had for this young lady in her boy's eyes and knew he cared deeply for this young woman. She did not express how she felt because it would kill her to see her boy upset if she admitted to him that it would never work out. Mr. Singh would not accept a white girl ever. She didn't mind him marrying a Caucasian girl, and in her heart, she knew Manny loved her.

Manny felt his mother genuinely understood him.

He said, "Thank you so much, mom, for supporting me. Do you want to meet her? I would love it if you met her."

"I am sure she is a very special lady, my boy. I will, my son, but not right now, maybe a little later."

"John is in heaven now. He told me to speak and follow my heart, so that's what I'm doing. He told me before he passed away to tell you and Papa. He said you would understand."

Manjot was silent and remembered what she always used to say when her boy was young, that she would let him live like a Canadian and not stand in the way of his heart. She was absolutely torn about what to do. She was confused and hurt about what was going to happen. She went upstairs to her room and started to cry. She looked at all the old photos of Manny. He was so happy when he was a kid—when he had a big smile while he was petting Toby, when he went to the beach, when he had his first puppy, even when he got himself ice cream. She said to herself that she would never stand in her son's way. But would the Indian tradition override her final decision? Her opinion would ultimately not matter due to the tradition of arranged marriages from generation to generation. She knew it would be impossible for Manny to marry this young white lady.

The next day after school, Manny brought Crystal over.

Manjot was in the kitchen, and Crystal said with a radiant smile, "Hi, Mrs. Singh! How are you doing?"

She gave Manjot a box of chocolates. Manjot was surprised. Manny looked at this beautiful, young lady who was talking to his mother and complimenting and hugging her. She told Manjot she was studying Sikhism and wanted to be with Manny all his life. Manjot appreciated and liked Crystal. She saw the love in Crystal's eyes for her son and that her little Manny was very happy seeing them bond.

Then, Mr. Singh pulled into the yard and walked in. He had come home early and saw Crystal standing there. He was in shock.

Manny said, "Papa, this is my girlfriend. I love her so much."

Mr. Singh was speechless. Crystal greeted Mr. Singh and walked up to give him a small hug and compliment his turban. Something happened to Mr. Singh. When he felt Crystal's shoulder on his, for a split second, he felt something powerful that he had never felt before. Crystal said that she was studying Sikhism and wanted to become a Sikh. After a few minutes, Mr. Singh nodded, speechless, and went directly into his bedroom. He was a little shocked at what Crystal said but didn't feel angry about it. There was a peaceful and good feeling about Crystal, he felt. It scared him that he felt this way. He went to bed early as he usually did. Manny and Crystal left shortly after to go bowling.

The next day, when Manny wasn't home, Mr. Singh came home from work, and Manjot was waiting for him at the dinner table.

Mr. Singh said, "I didn't want to say anything yesterday, but who invited her over?"

"Manny did," she said. "And I don't think Manny is ready to get married. He is very happy with his Caucasian girlfriend. He loves her so much; I see it in his eyes, I know. Do you think we should let them be together? I have a good feeling, and I like her. She seems very nice, caring, and beautiful. I really don't mind. I don't want to see my son get hurt."

Mr. Singh put his fist on the table and said, "Look, I told you before. I have known for quite some time that he has a girlfriend. Jarnal showed me pictures of them standing together, holding hands, and kissing."

Manjot blurted out, "Jarnal is a very bad man. He is causing trouble in our family, trust me."

"Trust you?" Mr. Singh said. "Just like you went to the beach that time, lying naked, hanging out with other men! Jarnal is my best friend; without him, we would be nothing. I was extremely upset. I wanted to teach our son a lesson by showing him some Indian discipline like a good slap to the face, but Jarnal explained to me that doesn't work in this country and asked me to trust him. So, I changed my approach. He told me not to get mad at Manny as he wouldn't listen to me. He told me to be nice to Manny and trust him, that Manny would fall into my hands and listen to me. I realized that Jarnal is a smart individual. He had an Indian girl in mind who was well-read and beautiful and was coming to Toronto soon, to his relatives. I looked at her picture and was impressed, and Jarnal suggested we get Manny married soon. Then we don't have to worry about him fooling around with white girls. He gave me the advice to move to Toronto, so Manny can have more career opportunities. He assured me I'd get severance pay from the mill until I start working at the steel mill in Toronto. I have worked so hard for our boy so he can have a good life. I don't want him to waste it. He is still young; he is just feeling this love now because it is his first experience. He will soon forget about the white girlfriend and be in love with the Indian wife we have picked out for him. I have planned for this, and we are moving to Toronto in two weeks on July 1st. Manny promised he is coming with us, and I am sure he will forget all about the girlfriend after being in Toronto for some time. He will love being in the big new city and being with his soon-to-be beautiful Indian wife. It's much better for his future. Think about it, really think about it. Don't listen to Kuljit. She is a wannabe white like her husband, and they are brainwashing you, and you watch too many white shows on the television. Get your act together. You know these women sleep around, are out with different guys. Then they want a divorce later. At first, they act nice, but later, they start to drink, smoke, be lazy, and don't work."

Manjot said, "How can you think like that? You haven't even given her a chance. Not all Caucasian women are the same, and same goes for the Indian women. Didn't you like her when you met her?"

Mr. Singh was speechless again. His feeling towards Crystal was unexplainable, and he didn't want to admit this to Manjot, but Manjot knew.

"See, you can't even admit you like her because you know in your heart that she is good, but just because she is Caucasian, you don't want to accept the relationship."

Mr. Singh nodded again.

Manjot said, "She is very kind, caring, and loving."

Mr. Singh said, "There you go again. There is no second-guessing. I don't care how I feel about Crystal, even if she is good. This is our Indian tradition. Manny has to marry his own kind. Case closed. We will start a second chapter in our new life with our new daughter-in-law and new house. She will take care of us. I am getting old. I want to retire soon, and we can travel back to India. Manny will have children, and I will set him up with a nice job in the steel factory. Our daughter-in-law will cook, clean, and take care of us. I am at an age that if something were to happen to me, you and Manny will be in good hands and with someone we can trust, one of our own. A good Indian girl will watch Indian movies with us, make us Indian sweets. My dear, you see my dream and vision is for the best. That's why I didn't get upset at Manny because he is a boy. Let him experience this so-called puppy love. He is feeling love? Don't worry, it's only temporary. Arranged marriage has been in our religion and culture for centuries. So, don't mess around with our culture. We know what will be better for him. He is a teenage boy. Don't fall for his feelings. Trust me, it's best for his future."

Manjot hated the proposal as Mr. Singh was laying it out and stormed into her bedroom. Arranged marriages had been part of the religion for centuries but her very own arranged marriage was a disaster, and she did not want it for Manny. She didn't agree with Mr. Singh's opinion that only a young Indian lady would understand the culture and the way things were done in an Indian family and take care of the family.

Manjot wanted Manny to be happy in the future. On the other hand, there might well be a culture clash if he married his Caucasian girlfriend. Maybe he *would* forget about her when they moved to Toronto. Manjot tried not to get emotionally involved in her son's feelings towards his girlfriend. She reminded herself that there was no guarantee of what would happen in the future with an arranged marriage. The Indian wife would never leave him because of their traditional values and stay committed to Manny for the rest of his life, as she was committed and loyal to Mr. Singh, even though she was in a bad relationship and unhappy because of that. He would eventually fall in love with his soon-to-be new Indian wife. Manny's arranged marriage had been in the works for two years, thanks to Jarnal mentioning that this well-educated, beautiful Indian girl was about to come to Canada soon and would be a perfect match for Manny. As happens in the culture, they knew of her through Jarnal's relatives in Toronto. A part of Manjot felt she had to stand by the centuries-old tradition of arranged marriage, no matter what.

Manjot wasn't looking forward to moving to Toronto for Manny's sake, even though she liked it there while on their vacation.

Kuljit came over for chai tea and cookies. She said she would fly to Toronto with Ravy for Manny's wedding. They were looking at a variety of Indian suits and dresses for the wedding and were trying to be excited about it.

Manjot said, "You are right, *saheli*! Maybe my son isn't ready to get married. He really loves his girlfriend."

Kuljit said, "That's why I'm not forcing or pressuring Ravy to marry yet."

Manjot felt conflicted and confused.

CHAPTER 18

The prom happened. The lovebirds had a good time dancing all night. Manny wore a black tuxedo, and Crystal wore a graceful prom dress. They attended the mountain party and enjoyed themselves with the students from all the other grades. School was finally over. Manny and Crystal took off to their favourite spot in the mountains, where they could see the stars shining at night, holding on to each other's souls and feeling as one.

Manny said to Crystal, "I love you more than anything in this world, but next week, my parents and I are going to Toronto to visit my sick uncle."

"Oh, no!" said Crystal, "I am sorry to hear that, my love. Manny, I love you more than anything on this Earth, and I want to be with you for the rest of my life. I can't stand being separated from you."

Manny said, "Same here, my shining star. I love you so much. I will be back very soon, like in a couple of weeks."

He gave her something that she could remember him by. It was a *kara*—a steel bracelet to symbolize that whatever a person does with their hands has to be in keeping with the advice given by God. Its circular shape symbolizes God as never-ending; it is a permanent bond with God and one's loved ones.

Manny gently slid the *kara* on Crystal's wrist and said, "When I'm gone, this will remind you of me because *you are my shining star day, and night. I love you, my love!*"

Crystal kissed the *kara* and said, "I will never forget you and will miss you all the time when you're not here close to me."

The Singhs had only three days left to pack for Toronto. Manny wondered why they were packing so much for a few days' visit.

He asked his mother, "Mom, why are you packing everything? We are just going for a couple of weeks, right?"

Manjot was silent. Manny asked if she was okay.

She paused and said, "Don't worry, son, I am packing some other things, just in case we might need them. You don't worry. Go spend time with your friends."

In her heart, she was feeling guilty about lying to her little boy.

"We will be leaving in a few days. Me and your Aunty Kuljit will pack your suitcases, okay?"

Manny looked at his mother and thought, "Yes! I don't have to pack anything," as a typical teenager of his age would think to get out of doing any work. "I will go over to Crystal's and hang out with her all day."

He wanted to spend as much time as possible with her before he left on the trip to Toronto.

Later that evening, Mr. Singh came back from work, and Manjot was still packing and dusting and thoroughly cleaning every window, ceiling, and floor.

Mr. Singh said, "Wow, great job, dear! You almost got everything packed up and cleaned. Nice! I have the delivery drivers to move all of our stuff on July 2nd. Jarnal has arranged it, and he will be staying here for a couple of nights to house sit and make sure they load up all our belongings carefully. He will get it hauled off in the moving vans to our new house in Toronto. And I have some other great news as well. Jarnal said he found us some tenants who will start renting our house from July 15th, so I am excited. He has also told me to take the last couple of days off from work to get the rental agreement done and take care of any financial needs. I have to get it all sorted out, and he said he will sell all our vehicles, including Manny's, and send us the money. So, I don't have to worry about it. He is also going to come to Manny's wedding in Toronto. He said he is so pleased to see us move on with our lives and settle in Toronto. I have all the respect for Jarnal. Without Jarnal, this would not have been possible, and he helped us out so much since the day we arrived in Canada. He is like a brother to me."

Manjot looked at Mr. Singh with a disgusted face as if she were about to puke. She always got a bad feeling from this man.

It was the last day before the move to Toronto. Kuljit and Ravy were at the Singh's house to say goodbye before they left. Then the red Chrysler pulled up to their house, and out came Jarnal. Manjot remembered that this car was following her at the beach and kept driving by her place. Jarnal walked into the house and sat down in the living room.

Manjot felt sick to her stomach and pointed out the car to Kuljit, when nobody was paying attention, and whispered to her, "That was the car from the beach that day, you see?"

Meanwhile, in the living room, Manny and Ravy were sitting in the family room with Jarnal and Mr. Singh. Jarnal was having some rye whisky and coke and was looking at Manny with a little smirk.

He said to Manny, "You are a little playboy, hey. You like to have fun I see? It's okay, I know what you were doing."

Manny was wondering why he was looking at him with a devilish smile as if he wanted him to get into some kind of trouble but then realized that he had seen Jarnal's car follow his car one day when he was with Ravy, Crystal, and Tina. Maybe that's what he was talking about as he smiled deviously.

Kuljit pulled Manjot into the kitchen and said that Jarnal was trying to push her to get Ravy married as well and felt a little weird about him because he warned her that Ravy would start dating white women.

She said, "He always seemed a bit creepy, and he tried to touch my hand and asked me to sleep with him a long time ago when Harry and I first came from India. He used to come over quite often and pretend that he was helping us. So, I was careful around that man and stayed away from him. I told Harry, and then he decided to quit the mill and became a realtor. We cut off any contact with him from then on. I didn't say anything at first because he is kind of related to you guys, but seeing him again in your house made me anxious, and I felt that I had to tell you."

Manjot replied, "When we were living at his house, he came downstairs when Mr. Singh was at work. He tried to hit on me by grabbing my hand and forcing me into the bedroom. His wife, Karm, was at work, and he would leave his work early when he knew I would be alone at home. It was horrible. I refused him many times, and he was extremely upset. Poor Manny was just a baby crying alone. His wife had no idea, and she was so nice to me. I wanted to get out of there and go back to India, but we had nowhere to go, being newcomers. I didn't want to tell my husband because he would have blamed me, saying I was slutty and that it was my fault. So, I kept quiet about it, and it kept going on till we moved out on our own. I felt so ashamed, and I blamed myself. I was very miserable. I would try not to stay by myself. I would lock myself and Manny in my room until my husband came home, or I would try to stay upstairs with Karm when she didn't go to work.

I would tell her to miss work on purpose, telling her I was scared or sick so someone would be with me. Thank God, I got out of his house. He tried to come over when I was at the new house, but I never let him inside and stayed clear of him. He finally stopped coming by after I told him to get lost."

Kuljit gave Manjot a big hug, saying, "May he burn in hell."

Manjot, with tears in her eyes, continued, "The car at the beach following us all makes sense now. He took pictures of us in our bathing suits and showed my husband. That is why he physically beat me up that night. I had kept this secret inside me for so many years, and now I am telling you, my *saheli*. We are flying out tomorrow, and I will miss you, my good friend."

Kuljit hugged her best friend and held her very tight and said, "He is an asshole, and it's not your fault. I can understand why you can't tell your husband. He is his best friend and thinks the world of Jarnal, and he won't believe you, and I agree with you that he might blame you. I can't stand him at all. I can't stay in the same room as him."

The next day, Jarnal drove them all to Vancouver International Airport to board the flight to Toronto. Manjot never looked at or spoke to Jarnal on the way. She stared out the window, even though he was trying to make eye contact with her through his rear-view mirror.

At the airport, Jarnal discussed his plans with Mr. Singh alone, out of the car, away from Mr. Singh's family. Manny was looking through the window while both of them were talking. Jarnal gave Mr. Singh a big hug and said that he would take care of Manny's girl problems for him. He assured him he was going to break the couple up and told him not to worry. Mr. Singh listened to his good friend and agreed with the plan. He made sure Manjot and Manny wouldn't know about it. The family boarded the flight to Toronto.

The next day, Jarnal met with Tom, Crystal's father. Tom had given his phone number to Mr. Singh when he came over to complain about his daughter drinking at their house while the Singhs were away during spring break. Jarnal and Tom went for a coffee, and Jarnal told Tom that Manny was going to marry an Indian girl and that he was never going to marry Crystal anyway. Tom was furious at what Manny had done to his daughter and knew from the start to never trust a coloured man. He wanted to beat the shit out of Manny, but at the same time, he was relieved that Manny was out of the picture now. Jarnal suggested Tom change his phone number and make sure Crystal didn't receive any mail from Manny. If any mail did come in from Manny, Tom should give it to Jarnal.

Jarnal said, "Tom, this is the way it's going to have to work. I know it's not right, but it is the only way for your daughter to get over him. She can move on."

Jarnal said, "In the end, she will have a white husband that you guys can like. She is beautiful; she will find someone else."

Tom smiled and was happy, but at the same time had qualms about going as far as keeping the mail from his daughter. Nevertheless, he went along with the plan.

He said, "Don't tell my wife; she is too sensitive, and I know my daughter will be heartbroken, but this is the only way. Thank you again, Jarnal."

They shook hands in agreement with the plan.

In Toronto, the Singh's relatives picked them up and drove them to their new house. The first thing Manny looked for was a phone. It had been so long since he had spoken to Crystal, but there was no phone at their house. Then he went over to Manjot's cousin's house, which wasn't too far away, and tried to use their phone. He excitedly dialed Crystal's number. The number was out of service. He unsuccessfully tried over and over again. Manny's face fell like a sad puppy's. He put his head down and walked back to his house.

A few days later, he said to his mother, "I want to go back home. I made a mistake coming here. Please can we go back? I am missing Crystal terribly. Where is this sick uncle, anyway?"

"I know you are missing your friends. We will leave soon, okay my beautiful son? Make your Papa happy by listening to him."

Manjot covered her eyes with a *chunni* and went into the washroom. She didn't want Manny to observe her. Tears rolled down her cheeks. She started crying, asking the gurus why this had to happen. Her son was hurting so much that she could feel his pain. She couldn't take it anymore and shut down.

Mr. Singh brought in Indian take-out and also got Manny a new surprise. It was a brand new Rolex. Manny opened it up and pretended to be excited.

Mr. Singh said to Manny, "My son, I love you. Listen to me, I am your father, and I love you very much."

He hugged Manny. Manny was not used to feeling any emotion or even a hug from his father. He was used to Mr. Singh ignoring him all his life when he was growing up in B.C.

CHAPTER 19

A week had passed. Crystal was wondering why Manny never called her and was missing him very much. Then Tom gave her a letter he said was from Manny. She started jumping up and down and was excited. It had a false address on it, and it said:

Crystal, I am sorry. I have decided to get married to an Indian girl. I no longer love you and have just used you. I always wanted to marry an Indian girl, so please leave me alone for life and don't send any letters.

Crystal burst into tears. She immediately went to her room and started throwing her things around. She started to hyperventilate. Dorothy came into the room and hugged her. Dorothy would never have thought in a million years that Manny would do such a thing since she had started to get to know him better over the years. She thought he was an honest and well-mannered boy.

Crystal was an emotional wreck. She cried all night and stayed in bed in her pyjamas. She didn't even eat because she was so upset.

Jarnal phoned Tom and asked him if Crystal received the letter he typed. He said yes she had and told him that his daughter was really upset and that he felt bad about his daughter's pain.

Jarnal told him that it was temporary, that she would find someone better, and that Manny was marrying an Indian girl anyway. Manny had sent a letter to Crystal, and Tom felt guilty that he did not give her the real letter. He simply put it aside.

Jarnal said he wanted Tom to give him any letters from Manny to Crystal. Tom thought it was weird that Jarnal wanted to personally read the letters.

Tom said, "Are you sure you want any letters that Manny has been sending?"

Jarnal said, "I have to read them to find out how he is doing there. Then I will send one to his address."

Tom never read the letter and didn't want to. He thought what Manny wrote was not his business and Jarnal was overstepping appropriate boundaries. But he kept quiet.

Jarnal read the fake letter he wrote to Crystal that was supposedly from Manny:

Hello, Crystal, I love you more than anything in the world, and I will be back soon. Just remember you are my shining star, day and night. I love you so much. I keep thinking about you all day and night. I can't sleep, eat, or talk because I miss you so badly. I want to be with you for the rest of my life.

Jarnal chuckled and told Tom that Manny was a turban twister mumma's boy.

Tom was feeling guilty about the situation and didn't like Jarnal's comments.

"Look, I didn't think he really loved my daughter, but maybe he did. And she definitely loved him back. So, let's not make any fun of this situation. I don't like doing this. If he is getting married, I don't understand why he is still sending love letters."

"He will stop soon," said Jarnal. "Look, here are the wedding invitations. Manny is really getting married. He was playing with Crystal's heart and only using her. He didn't really love her."

Jarnal typed a letter to Manny pretending to be Crystal and sent it to Toronto. He told Mr. Singh to make sure he received it first and then give it to Manny.

When the letter arrived, Mr. Singh gave the mail to Manny and pretended he didn't know who it was from. Manny ran upstairs, excited to open it. It said,

> *You are my shining star, day and night, not anymore. I have decided to move on with my new boyfriend, Chris. I love him so much. I don't love you. You are brown, and I am white. It is never gonna work out between us, so stop sending me letters and move on with your life. Don't ever try to call me either. I have changed my phone number so you will stop calling me. Please leave me alone. I am with someone else who makes me happy. Remember never to call me or send me any more letters.*

Manny was in tears and shaking badly. Manjot had no idea what had happened and held him. He cried all day, and even after that, he was emotionally distraught. He was in his bedroom thinking about Crystal and how they used to spend time together at lunch and at her house, how her perfume smelled when they first met, her beautiful face and her green eyes and auburn hair, seeing her beside him for the first time in high school, making love for the first time.

Manjot felt devastated that her little boy was feeling so miserable. It was killing her inside. She tried everything to cheer him up, but nothing worked. Later on, she started taking anti-depressants because she was so depressed, which resulted in Mr. Singh accusing her of being weak, not smart enough, lazy, emotionless, and crazy.

Three weeks had gone by. The moving trucks brought the furniture as Jarnal had promised. Mr. Singh was working at his new job at the steel factory and got Manny a job there as well, but all Manny kept asking about was when they were going back. Mr. Singh tried everything to lift his son's spirits. He bought him a new car, treated him to dinner, and told him to go hang out with his cousins. But it didn't help. He was depressed and missed Crystal very much. Nothing seemed to snap Manny out of this state. The letters eventually would stop coming soon after too. He wrote one more letter to Crystal demanding she call him and talk over the phone, but that letter never made it to her at all. Tom gave it to Jarnal, and he kept it. Tom made sure that Jarnal got every letter from Manny that came into his house.

Crystal wasn't faring any better. She experienced a depressive state that lasted a long time. She wasn't happy or motivated to do anything anymore. Dorothy felt bad for her daughter and tried to make her happy by telling her to go out with other boys, but it wasn't the same. She was never the same. She carved Manny's name in her arm with a knife to prove that she loved him so much. Crystal converted to Sikhism and wore an Indian suit, turban, and Manny's *kara*. Tom asked her why she was wearing her steel bracelet. She said that it connected her to Manny, and the *kara* was a symbol linked to the guru and other Sikhs and truth and honesty and restraint and gentleness. Chants of "*Waheguru! Waheguru! Waheguru!*" came every day from her bedroom in the morning and night. Dorothy was amazed at how intensely her daughter was interested in Sikhism.

Jarnal was encouraging Mr. Singh to quickly get all the wedding invitations ready and book the hall for Manny's wedding.

He said, "Let's get it done in a couple of months. I am going to India to meet the girl and her family. She will be coming soon."

Jarnal went to India to talk with the girl's parents and told them that she was going to marry into a nice family. He also told them that they had property and that the boy was smart and good looking, so they agreed to the match. Jarnal received $20,000 from the girl's parents for arranging the match so she could come to Canada. He returned to Canada shortly after. The Singhs had no idea that Jarnal was given money for arranging the match, and the parents of the girl never mentioned it.

The girl finally moved to Toronto, staying at the house of one of Jarnal's relatives. The Singhs went there to meet her. She was very beautiful and wore Indian bangles and a red *saree*. She wore little makeup and was very polite, respectful, and charming to Mr. Singh. He fell in love with her and found her perfect to be his daughter-in-law.

After two months, Manny seemed even more distant from everybody. His face was always sad.

Then, the morning came when Mr. Singh told Manny to wear a red turban and black suit *because he was going to get married the next day*. To Manny, this news was surreal. Marriage the next day? Was he dreaming? He hadn't even met or seen his bride yet, but he was supposed to spend the rest of his life with a stranger . . . and love her!

His emotions were a boiling cauldron of shock, anger, apprehension, and resignation. He decided to go along with it because he didn't think he had a choice, and he didn't have Crystal anyway, so did it matter who he married? He was also influenced by seeing his father so happy, and, surprisingly, a part of him wanted to please Mr. Singh.

The night before the wedding, the couple participated in a ritual called *Maiyaan*. It's an Indian tradition to be performed just before marriage. A mixture of turmeric, oil, and water is applied to the face and skin. It is normally performed by the female cousins or sisters of the person getting married. Then, his cousins danced all night at the *Maiyaan*. Manny observed all his female relatives dancing and putting on the *haldi*. He was in a dream-like state and sat motionlessly.

There were so many people. Kuljit and Ravy were invited but couldn't make it to the wedding. Ravy had become a drug addict, lost connection with his parents and friends, and moved to the lower mainland. He was now living with cousins. Kuljit and her husband had also moved away from the small town to the mainland.

Meanwhile, Crystal's condition wasn't getting any better. She hadn't heard from Manny in months. She never left her room and was in the worst shape of her life, emotionally. Her mother was concerned.

One night, amid her tears, Crystal noticed something bright outside. She walked up to the window and saw the same star that she and Manny used to see. She opened the window and started speaking to the star.

She said, "You are my shining star, day and night. I love you."

As she said it, she felt a surge of energy and euphoria, as if she had just talked to Manny and felt his kiss. It was as if she could feel him surrounding her and his love for the star shining very bright. She couldn't explain it; she just wanted to feel the love the star reflected.

Manny would dream of Crystal at night and would also look up in the skies to see the stars. He would remember how they used to go to their special place in the mountains and would say, "You are my shining star, day and night. I love you."

This also uplifted Manny. Looking at the stars reminded him of Crystal.

CHAPTER 20

On his wedding day, Manny wore his brand new red turban and Indian suit with his Rolex watch. Mr. Singh looked sharp in his new turban and suit. His cousins were also dressed up. Manjot was wearing a brand new *saree* with gold ornaments. They arrived in a limo and went up to the *Gurudwara*. They sat on the ground in front of the Guru and behind the bride and groom. Beside Manny was his bride, Sonjot. She was wearing a beautiful red *saree*, and her face was covered by her *chunni*.

Then the ceremony began. They walked around the Guru Granth Sahib four times, praying with Sonjot, holding an Indian cloth. Then they sat down, and the *Buba* gave them the blessing to be a happily married couple. After the ceremonies, they all went downstairs to the *langar* to eat. Jarnal was the first one there. He was wearing a blue pinstriped suit with brand new dress shoes.

He said to Manny, "I wish you the very best with your new wife. You are making your dad so proud."

Manny didn't like Jarnal's remark and walked away. He wasn't impressed by him at all, but after a while, he asked him, "Uncle, can I come back home with you for a week? I want to say bye to my friends."

Jarnal grabbed Manny's arm, took him to one side, and called him an idiot.

"Don't play games. I know you want to go to the white girl's house. She is going out with another boy. I have seen them in the playground, holding hands, kissing, and hugging. Don't be a moron. She doesn't love you."

He told Manny to go back to his wife.

Then, he went up to Sonjot and said, "Make sure you take good care of this young man and his family. Welcome to the new family."

They took pictures outside with each other and went back home. They had to get ready for the reception at night, and all Manny could see was how happy his father was. He was shaking hands with everyone, he was laughing, and all the relatives were congratulating Mr. Singh. The guests started to drink. Jarnal was also drinking, dancing, doing the *bhangra* with Mr. Singh and telling him how his life was going to be so much better.

At the reception, everybody was dancing and drinking; the party lasted into the wee hours of the morning. Mr. Singh and Jarnal had a few too many drinks and fell asleep on the couch.

The newly married bride and groom went home. It was extremely awkward for Manny because someone else was in his bedroom sleeping with him. He didn't even know her and didn't do anything sexual with her because all he kept thinking about was Crystal.

He thought to himself, "What did I get myself into? Who is this person sleeping next to me? Is she my wife? I have no feelings for her. I don't know her. This is beyond awkward. Is this for real? I'm married to her for the rest of my life and supposed to love her. Is this what I am supposed to do? I don't even want to make love to her."

He was very confused, but he supposed he would somehow have to learn how to make a traditional Indian arranged marriage work.

A few weeks had passed, and Sonjot was trying to get used to her new family. Mr. Singh was still excited. He had a daughter-in-law who was going to take care of the house, cook and clean, and take care of Manny as a good housewife, just as Mr. Singh's wife did. Manjot was showing her how to do all the household duties as she had been taught when she arrived from India. Manny was working with his father at the steel factory. They would work together all day and would come home at the same time from work, and Sonjot would make supper for everyone since Manjot was working night shifts cleaning houses. Mr. Singh absolutely adored his new daughter-in-law, praising her for how she made dinner and how good it tasted and complimenting her for doing all the housework. Manny observed that his relationship with his father was solid since he respected his father's wishes and got married. Mr. Singh was always happy and bought Manny many new things, not the least a new car for the couple. Sonjot received an expensive gold jewellery set from her father-in-law and mother-in-law, which she kept in her bedroom closet.

After the couple had been married for a few months, Manjot was wondering where Sonjot was going every day for a few hours during the day. In a rude way, Sonjot told her she was going to the library and not to worry. Manjot didn't approve of Sonjot leaving without telling her where she was going. This feud continued until one day, when the men were at work, Sonjot told Manjot to shut up and pushed her. Manjot couldn't believe it and started yelling at Sonjot. The same night, when the men came back from work, Manjot confronted Sonjot, and the women started arguing in front of Manny and Mr. Singh. Then Mr. Singh told Manjot to be quiet and to not fight with Sonjot. He told Sonjot that Manjot was sometimes out of line and crazy and that Sonjot was right. Sonjot smiled and went to her bedroom.

Manjot couldn't believe Mr. Singh took Sonjot's side. Manjot told him and Manny that Sonjot kept going out during the day without telling him or her, and nobody knew where she was going. Manny didn't say anything about the situation but let his father speak about it. Mr. Singh said that it was ok, and Manjot was overreacting. Manjot was upset at Mr. Singh for not taking it seriously because in their own relationship, when Manny was young and they were new to Canada, Manjot was never allowed anywhere and was physically beaten if she disobeyed Mr. Singh. However, since Manny was married, it was okay for Sonjot to do anything she wanted. This would be the start of many squabbles between Manjot and her new daughter-in-law about things such as folding laundry and cleaning the house the right way. Manjot didn't feel Sonjot was listening to her and felt disrespected by her daughter-in-law.

Sonjot left home again without saying anything. This time, Manjot followed her and noticed she would go to the payphone and talk on the phone for a long time. Then, Manjot walked right up to Sonjot and grabbed the phone. Sonjot snatched the phone back from her, put the phone down, and told her that she was talking to her mother. Then, Manjot asked for the phone to check who she was talking to, and Sonjot threw it at Manjot. The tension between the ladies escalated over time, but in Mr. Singh's eyes, Sonjot was an angel. Sonjot was innocent and special to him. He even gave her access to and signing authority of his bank account.

Sonjot wanted to go out with Manny. She wanted to see the city and kept asking him to go to various places and events, but

Manny was never in the mood to go out. However, because they hadn't gone anywhere for their honeymoon, Mr. Singh insisted that Manny take her out and gave him money. He told him to take her to the most beautiful restaurant and to get a hotel room for a few days for the honeymoon.

Manny listened to his father and drove Sonjot in their new car to Montreal, where they got a hotel room and drank and partied at the nightclub all night. Manny got drunk. At the hotel, Sonjot made a special drink and crushed some pills into it. She told Manny to drink it, and it knocked him out. The next day, he wasn't feeling well at all. He was dazed and had a hangover. However, Sonjot insisted they drink more and go out for dinner and then to the clubs. They did it all over again—and again that night, when Manny was intoxicated, Sonjot crushed some more pills into his drink without him knowing. The side-effects from the drugs this time made him wilder and hyperactive and out of control at the clubs. Manny didn't know what he was doing, and he started drinking hard shots, smoking pot, and doing lines of cocaine with his new wife. She also partied as he did.

The newlyweds continued this trend in the weeks ahead. Manny started to drink after work now and spent hours in bars by himself. It affected his work and relationship with his mother and father because he became distant as he kept indulging.

Sonjot told Mr. Singh that it was ok for Manny to hang out with his cousins, because Manny never had a sibling when he was younger. Sonjot said she understood that he was enjoying his new freedom, and she was okay with it.

Sonjot said, "He is married to me. He is my husband. Dad, please relax and let me handle him."

Mr. Singh, with a big smile, said, "You're right. He is grown up, and he can make his own decisions with you, and when you have children, I can retire, and your mom can too. Guru gave me a blessing when you came into our lives. I am so grateful for you. You will take over the house with my son."

Manjot was looking at her daughter-in-law and then looked at Mr. Singh with an expression he had never seen on his wife's face, and Mr. Singh felt a cold chill through his body.

Manjot looked at Sonjot and said, "My boy is pretty much drunk every night. How come you don't try to stop him? I am concerned for him."

Sonjot replied, "Let him explore. He has been sheltered all his life. Let him have experience and be a man. Don't worry about it; he is married to me. Stop babying him, and stop interfering."

Mr. Singh said, "Enough, Manjot, we will not interfere anymore; let them be a couple and work it out on their own. She is right! He is married and a grown man. He is not our responsibility anymore; he is Sonjot's."

Manjot stormed into her room and regretted that her little boy got married to this spoiled brat and blurted out that he should have married the white girl back home and that Sonjot showed very little sympathy and that she didn't have respect for her or her boy. But Mr. Singh laid down the law, and Manjot had to listen.

After a few weeks, Mr. Singh started to feel concerned for Manny. All of a sudden, he had started showing up late to work, and he was always drinking and going out to party, but Mr. Singh kept it to himself and asked Manny to drink less. He never mentioned to Manjot that maybe she was right. Manny didn't listen to anyone; his heart was somewhere else, and he wanted to kill his pain.

One day, he went uninvited to a house party where he got too intoxicated, and the people at this house party barely knew Manny. He was by himself and stumbled upon the party after someone at the club mentioned it to him. He was so extremely drunk and high that he walked into the washroom and fell flat in the bathtub. A few people at the party saw Manny lying in the tub, passed out. They started making fun of him, asking one another if they knew who this turban twister was. Nobody had a clue, so a few of them sat Manny up in the bathtub. They pulled down his pants, put shaving cream on his face and eyebrows, and started to shave his face and eyebrows right off. Then some drunk men dumped beer all over his turban, and a crowd formed. They were howling and making loud noises. They each began taking turns urinating on Manny, making fun of his skin and turban. Then one reveller pulled off Manny's turban, and his hair came flying out. They grabbed a razor, gave him a buzz cut, and then completely shaved his head. They tied his feet together with the turban, and when Manny woke up the next day, hungover, he noticed his legs were tied, and he couldn't recall where he was. He tried walking back home, smelling like booze, faeces, and urine, with his pants on backwards and shirt ripped, with part of his turban wrapped around his leg, with his wallet lost, and his hair cut. He was also missing a shoe.

His vision blurry, he stumbled to the nearest liquor store, grabbed a bottle of vodka with the money he had in his front pocket and sat in the parking lot all by himself, drinking the whole bottle. He was washing away the pain of his love for Crystal.

He was crying for her, calling out her name, "Crystal, Cryyyst-taaal, Crystttaaaal!".

He was on his hands and knees, and his face was towards the sky. A white lady came over to see how he was; she reminded him of Crystal. He tried to hug her, telling her how much he loved her with one arm over her shoulder as she bent over trying to see if he was okay.

He kept saying, "You're here, you're here. I love you so much," and kept calling her Crystal.

He smelled the same perfume that Crystal used to wear in high school when he first met her.

Manny fell over onto his back. Saliva was drooling from the side of the mouth, and his eyes began feeling heavy and opening and shutting slowly. The young woman, understanding the situation, became extremely worried and called the ambulance to help Manny get home because he was very intoxicated. As she waited for the ambulance, the police also arrived.

When she tried to give Manny water, he grabbed onto her leg and said, "Don't leave! Don't leave me."

He was in such deep emotional pain that he was crying loudly, saying that he missed his shining star. The woman felt bad for him.

She bent over and gave him a small hug, saying, "You will be fine."

Tears shone in the woman's eyes. She had a good heart and assumed the pain he was feeling was too much for him to bear. When she held on and said that everything was going to be all right, Manny stopped crying. He felt pure emotion and love from this lady, a feeling that he hadn't experienced in a while. It was as if someone cared about his pain and what he was going through. He started to hyperventilate but calmed down as she was hugging him and making sure he remained conscious.

CHAPTER 21

While all of this was going on across the street, Sonjot was observing everything and was smiling about it. She loved what was going on, like a true psychopath, enjoying the pain of others, and she did not even bother to come over to help Manny. She was laughing at him because his turban was gone, and he was crying on the street like a baby. She had wanted him to screw up and stay on drugs. But this situation was even better—there would be more turmoil in the family because his turban was gone, and Mr. Singh would have his head. She walked away to the payphone, as she always did almost every day at this particular time, to make a call to India again, but this time, she was more excited than usual.

A young man answered the call and said, "Sonjot, I love you, and I can't wait till you come back."

Sonjot said, "I love you too, my love! I will be coming back shortly. Our plan is working really well. In some time, I'll get Canadian citizenship, and then we can move to anywhere in the world, my love. Manny has started drinking heavily and is on drugs. Guess what? Someone cut off his turban when he was drunk. Haha! It's perfect! Soon I will be drugging that bitch, Manjot, and his stupid-ass big freak father too. I have gotten access to their bank accounts and have signing authority as well. They also have good life insurance, and it will come to us. We can be settled in India or anywhere in the world, my love. So, in the meantime, hang in there. I will soon be back, and we can start a life together. The big goof Mr. Singh is going back to B.C. to sell his old house next week. That's when I will make the move back to India. I will tell them that my mother is sick, and then I will never come back. I'll withdraw all their money and fly back home. They will never know what hit them. Hahaha! Anyway, I should be heading back home now. I want to see that loser get in trouble with his parents and really add fuel to the fire. Bye, my love! I will call you tomorrow."

Raj, Sonjot's boyfriend, said, "Love you! Keep fucking up their family. I can't believe someone cut off his turban! Hahaha!"

Sonjot rushed home and saw the police trying to take Manny inside after he refused to go into the ambulance. He couldn't even walk. The woman who had helped Manny was observing from her car outside and decided to get out and help Manny back to the house, but the officers told her to stay back. Manjot saw her baby boy standing there with police officers holding him up. She rushed outside and came to his aid. She held him like he was her little boy and noticed his turban was off and his hair was shaved. She immediately brought him inside and lay him on his bed. He kept mumbling Crystal's name. Then he saw his mother and burst out crying. She gave him water and tried to get him to sleep. Sonjot went inside the house and pretended to cry and act like she hadn't seen it all. Manjot told her to take care of Manny while she called a doctor.

The white woman who had helped Manny knocked on the door to tell Manjot what had happened and suggested he go to the hospital. But Sonjot grabbed the phone from Manjot and told everyone not to overreact. Manny was just drunk. Manjot didn't listen to Sonjot and wanted to call the doctor. Manny suddenly vomited, and Manjot came rushing over to help her son, while Sonjot just stood there. Sonjot said she would make supper for Mr. Singh while Manjot took care of Manny. She told the white girl to leave and that the situation wasn't her business.

Sonjot walked into the kitchen, grabbed more pills, and crushed them in the *lassi*. She stirred a glass for Mr. Singh and Manjot.

As soon as Mr. Singh came home, he saw his beautiful daughter-in-law, and the first thing she asked was, "Hi, Dad, how was your day at work?"

Mr. Singh replied, "Good, *beta!*"

Sonjot grabbed the *lassi* and gave it to Mr. Singh with his dinner. He asked where Manny was, and she said he was in the bedroom, resting with Manjot.

Then, Sonjot said to him, "Please, drink your *lassi*. You work very hard."

Obliging her, Mr. Singh drank his *lassi* and finished his dinner. Fifteen minutes later, he started feeling very angry and on edge.

Sonjot noticed the drugs were taking effect and decided that it was the best time to tell Mr. Singh what had happened.

She said, "Manny cut his hair today and got in trouble with the police. He was doing drugs as well. You have to stop him."

Mr. Singh was enraged that his son cut his hair. Under the influence of the drugs, he walked into Manny's room with his hands shaking in anger. He grabbed Manjot and pushed her aside. With a combination of adrenaline and fear, Manjot got up to tackle Mr. Singh, and they both hit the floor. He told Manny to get out of the house. Manny started swearing at Mr. Singh and left the house.

When he was leaving, Mr. Singh shouted, "Why did you cut off your turban?"

Mr. Singh gathered himself and, still influenced by the drugs in his system, tried to follow Manny. Manny drunkenly walked in the middle of the street, slipped down some steps, landed on his head, and fell unconscious. Sonjot stood in the kitchen smiling at what was happening and enjoying tearing the family to shreds. Manjot ran to where Manny was and called for an ambulance immediately to take him to the hospital. Her little boy didn't respond to her, and she was desperately trying to wake him up. The next day, Manjot was still in the hospital with Manny, making sure he wasn't alone.

Mr. Singh came back from work, and Sonjot was home alone. He asked her how Manny was. Mr. Singh was very worried about his boy and thought about him all day at work. He was also worried about his wife Manjot as well.

He asked, "Did you go to the hospital?"

Sonjot said, "No, Dad, I think he is fine. I thought I would stay home and take care of the chores. I'm sure they will be back soon."

Mr. Singh was worried about his family and wanted to visit them in the hospital, but Sonjot told him to relax at home. She said that she would go if he wanted her to. He should just rest at home as he had to go to work the next day. Mr. Singh left immediately for the hospital, disregarding what his daughter-in-law said. That was his son lying in the hospital, and he was very concerned about his health and well-being.

Manjot came back home and said to Sonjot, "Manny had to stay in the hospital and get his head checked out; he is still unconscious."

Sonjot apologized to Manjot. Manjot felt uneasy about Sonjot's motives and did not accept her apology. Manjot told her that she should have done something sooner about Manny's drug and drinking problem and that she didn't trust her anymore.

Mr. Singh took the day off work because he was very concerned that his son was in a coma and decided to take Manjot back to the hospital. Sonjot said she would stay home and make them something to eat for when they got back. She said that it would traumatize her to see Manny in such a condition.

Mr. Singh and Manjot waited in the hospital to see their son. Mr. Singh broke down and said that he couldn't believe what he had done to his wife and son, and he should have paid more attention to their son and listened to his wife Manjot. Mr. Singh was hurt and blamed himself. He started praying to the gurus to make his son regain consciousness.

The doctor came out and said, "We had to completely shave his head to assess the damage. He is in an acute coma, and we had to do more tests. We also had to get him detoxed as he had a very high blood–alcohol level and had heroin and cocaine in his system."

Mr. Singh, bawling his eyes out, went to Manny, held him, cried, and started praying. Manjot was there holding his hand as well. They prayed all night. The next day, Mr. Singh left the hospital for work. He was thinking about his son all day but soon had to leave for B.C. to sell their house because he had a good offer, and Jarnal told him to sell it as soon as possible; the price would fall if he waited.

The same night, he explained to his daughter-in-law that he wanted to cancel the trip to B.C. and stay with his son and wife until he got better. Sonjot convinced him to go and sell the house and that she would take care of Manjot and Manny—that's what she was there for—and that he wouldn't be gone long anyway. She said she wanted to get Manny sober and clean because he had a drug problem. She lied to Mr. Singh that she was pregnant and suggested that if anything ever happened to him and his wife, Sonjot should be the beneficiary of the life insurance policy. She told Mr. Singh that Manny would just blow the money on drugs and drinking, she wanted the best for his grandchild, and she cared about everyone. Mr. Singh agreed to everything that Sonjot was saying.

Back in B.C., Crystal woke up screaming. Dorothy ran into her bedroom and asked her what she had been dreaming about. Crystal said she didn't know; she was frightened by something. She tried to go back to sleep but couldn't. She was thinking of Manny. Something felt very different to Crystal, and she couldn't ignore the powerful feeling. She said to her mother that she felt Manny was nearby, and she felt his presence. Dorothy too felt a chill.

The next day, Tom was driving by the Singh's old house and noticed an old lady beside their house, on the ground. He went over, saw it was Bertha, and helped her up. Bertha thanked Tom but didn't recognize him.

However, Tom recognized Bertha and said, "I remember getting my car fixed by your husband. He was a good mechanic. Oh, and my daughter used to date that Indian kid, Manny. He lived beside you."

She looked at Tom, surprised, moved back into her walker and said, "Manny is a wonderful kid. I have so many memories of that boy coming to pet my dog every day and coming up for lunch. I have seen him grow up in front of me, and John would always show him how to fix cars and all kinds of things, even how to ride a bike. He was a genuine kid. My husband always used to say he had the heart of a lion, and when you fall off your bike you rooooarr! Get back on your bike and start to ride no matter how much pain you feel with a smile on your face. But you know, I haven't heard from him since he moved away, and he didn't say much and poof! They were outta that house, and soon all the moving trucks were here taking all the furniture and belongings too. And my health hasn't been that great. I just stay upstairs, and I can barely see and write, and I can't get around very well without my wheelchair or walker. My daughter comes by once in a blue moon to give me a hand but hasn't for months because of where she lives. Other than that, I sit around all day watching television. Oh, Tom, can you do me a big favour? Can you please go to my mailbox for me and grab my mail? That's what I was trying to do. I keep forgetting about it. I meant to tell my daughter, but I forgot . . . old age!"

Tom didn't hesitate and grabbed the mail for Bertha. She had several pieces of mail and asked Tom if he could open one letter and read it to her. Tom opened the letter. It read:

Dear Bertha,

Thank you for everything you and John have done in my life. I love you guys like my second parents. I wanted to say I am not happy here in Toronto. My parents forced me to come out here and tricked me. They are getting me to have an arranged marriage with someone I don't even know or love. I hate what they did to me. Can you please give this letter to Crystal? For some reason, her phone number doesn't work anymore. I just need to speak with her, Bertha. I love her more than anything in this world. This is my new address and phone number in Toronto.

To Crystal,

I can understand you moved on with your new boyfriend, Chris, and you never wanted me to write to you again, but

I am sick every day because I love my one and only love, Crystal. I have a hard time sleeping, eating, and even staying here. I want to be in your arms. You are my shining star, day and night. I love you for life, my love! I will come back to you someday to hopefully marry you, my love. I will never forget you.

Thank you so much again, Bertha. I love you, and please let her know and tell her I love her for eternity.

Bertha said to Tom, "I can't go anywhere. Can you please let your daughter know what was in the letter? Can you promise me that you will do that for me? Manny is a very nice boy. I practically raised him. He was like a son to me and John. He is a very nice boy who grew up into a gentleman."

Tom said that he would give Crystal the letter. He was hesitant but felt emotional about the letter, as if a spirit from the stars had passed through him. He also felt ashamed about how he treated Manny and how Jarnal had lied to him. He didn't want to have anything to do with Jarnal anymore. He felt the letter was from Manny's heart, and he loved his daughter. Tom felt that enough was enough. However, he needed time to work up the courage to hand the letter over to Crystal.

A few days later, Tom heard that Bertha had died in her sleep the day after giving him the letter. An emotional Tom felt he had to finally hand over the letter and come clean. He told Crystal about everything he had done, and that he was very sorry, and that Jarnal had lied to him. She was extremely upset at her father but more upset at Jarnal. After a few hours, she grudgingly praised her father for having the courage to at least tell her the truth.

Crystal was ecstatic and decided she had no time to be angry. After she read the letter, she didn't wait for a second to phone Manny. Crystal kept phoning, and nobody was answering the phone. She kept trying to call.

Sonjot was home and heard the phone ring but didn't bother answering it because she already had been to the bank and withdrawn $30,000 from Mr. Singh's account. She wanted to empty the account, but the bank manager said that Mr. Singh had to be there personally to withdraw the remaining $20,000 and ask Sonjot if they should call Mr. Singh about the rest of the money. But Sonjot refused and told the bank she would take the $30,000 only. The bank manager was suspicious and asked her what it was for. She said her mother was ill and the Singhs knew about it. She put the money in her suitcase ready to fly to India the next day.

Sonjot called her boyfriend from the house since nobody else was there and told him how excited she was that she was going back to India to be with him again in a very short time. And Raj couldn't wait either. He said that when Sonjot came back home, they were going to move to Australia with the money, purchase a house, and start a new life there.

Manjot arrived at the hospital. She forgot about the glass of *lassi* Sonjot had prepared for her, spiked with drugs, and left it in the car. She spent the rest of the night holding on to Manny's hand. Since he was still in a coma, she prayed and kept praying all night for Manny, holding on to her little boy's hand.

Mr. Singh landed at Vancouver International Airport with a bottle of fresh *lassi* his daughter-in-law packed for him. Then he drove the rented car from the mainland to the small town in northern B.C., his former home. He had the *lassi* in his lap but decided to drink it later. Finally, with 25 minutes to go before he reached his destination, he drank the *lassi* with one big swig.

When he was about five minutes away from the town, he slammed into a semi-truck while coming through an intersection. Mr. Singh had fallen asleep and driven through the red light. The semi-truck hit his rented car on the passenger side, and it spun around and slammed into a pole. Emergency crews arrived immediately on the scene, and Mr. Singh was transported to the hospital in the ambulance. The driver of the semi-truck escaped with minor injuries.

CHAPTER 22

Early the next morning, Sonjot, with her belongings packed and suitcases full of the Singh's money, called a taxi driver to take her to the airport. The phone was ringing. Sonjot saw that Manjot was calling from the hospital and decided not to answer the phone. Then, Manjot decided to go home to see what was happening because there was no answer. She noticed Sonjot wasn't home, and all the cupboards in her room were open and empty.

Since she was so tired, she drank the *lassi* that was in the fridge. Within 15 minutes, she began to feel dizzy, her legs gave out, and she collapsed, with feeling only in her upper body. She tried to drag herself to the phone and kept thinking about her little boy, Manny, who was in a coma, and knew she had to get to the phone so she could call for help. The drugs were having a severe effect on her nervous system, and she collapsed onto her elbows. She closed her eyes and lay on the floor. The only thing she could hear was her heartbeat.

At the airport, Sonjot bought some gifts for Raj and called him one last time before boarding the plane to tell him she had bought him a Rolex. However, it was the same watch that Mr. Singh had bought his son when he got married. It was worth $500. She took it off of Manny's hand when he was knocked out and kept it when the fight happened at the house. She briefly went into the washroom to put makeup on. She also bought expensive perfume and cologne for herself and Raj.

She was on the plane with all her gifts and money and was excited to go back home. Then, as she sat down in the seat, a little boy with a turban sat beside her, and his mother sat beside him. He must have been around nine years old and had the most adorable smile and beautiful big, brown eyes.

He was moving his arms and saying, "I'm Superman! I'm Superman!"

Sonjot smiled and said hello to the little boy. The little boy shyly turned to his mother and put his head on her shoulder.

His mother said, "He is a very active boy but sometimes very shy."

Sonjot said, "That's okay!" and tried to ignore them as the plane took off. While the stewardess was serving drinks, Sonjot took a brief nap with her head turned away from the young boy and his mother. All of a sudden, the young boy spilt Coke all over Sonjot's hair and new dress and started laughing. She woke up, furious, swearing at the little boy and his mother. His mother held her son and apologized. The little boy was scared and didn't speak after that. Then Sonjot went into the washroom to clean herself up, still angry at the boy. She came back and started swearing at the little boy again, and he started crying. The flight attendant asked Sonjot to go to the back of the plane, but she didn't want to do so. She argued with the flight attendant that she should stay in her seat and that the boy and his mother should move. Then the captain decided that she should move to the back because other passengers were complaining about her swearing so much. She was removed from her seat and escorted to the new seat at the back of the plane. She was worried about her luggage, and the crew assured her it was safe.

Back in Toronto, Manny was still in a coma, Manjot was passed out in the house, and Mr. Singh was admitted to the emergency room in his old town. The phone kept ringing and ringing at the Singh's house in Toronto, and then Manjot somehow emerged from her drug-induced stupor, crawled towards the phone, and answered it.

Manjot was still confused and dizzy from the drugs. It was Crystal on the other end of the line, and she asked, "Hi, is Manny there?"

Manjot said, "He is in the hospital. Call 911. Something is happening to me. Please help me!"

Crystal called the local ambulance for the Singh's house. They arrived at the house and took Manjot to the hospital. Drugs were found in her system, and they gave her an IV.

Crystal, worried about Manny and his mother, told her father what had happened, and he said that Jarnal told him that Manny's father was also in the local hospital in B.C. because he had been in a car accident. She immediately made arrangements to buy a ticket to Toronto for the next day, but for now, she went to the hospital to visit Mr. Singh.

Mr. Singh had no feeling in his legs and felt very vulnerable. For the first time in his life, he had to put his guard down. Jarnal was outside on the payphone, and then he saw Crystal walk into the room. Jarnal couldn't believe his eyes. It was Crystal in a white Indian suit and turban and the steel *kara* on her arm. She kneeled down and prayed. She held on to Mr. Singh's hands. Mr. Singh felt the warmth and love coming from this white Sikh lady and accepted her love. He saw the *kara* on her wrist and knew she was genuine because whatever a person does with their hands has to be in keeping with the advice given by the guru. *Waheguru* refers to the almighty God, supreme soul, the creator in Sikhism. *Wahe* (wondrous) + *guru* (teacher), together reveal the meaning of the word. He is the wondrous lord or teacher who dispels the darkness of ignorance and bestows the light of truth, knowledge, and enlightenment.

Crystal held on to Mr. Singh's hand, and he felt the love and kindness flow towards his weak body and soul. Tears flowed from his eyes, and he told her that Manny was in a coma. She started to cry and hugged Mr. Singh, praying *Waheguru, Waheguru*. After spending a few hours with Mr. Singh, trying to take care of him, she told him that he was going to Toronto the next day. The nurses told her that Mr. Singh had to rest, and visiting hours were over. Her father was right beside her.

She walked out and saw Jarnal still standing there, with his eyes wide open, looking at her as if he had just seen a ghost. She blasted him for what he had done to her and the Singhs and how he ruined all their lives, kicked him in the shin, and told him he was dirt and a scumbag. She said that she wished he would burn in hell, and she then spat in his direction.

Jarnal was surprised, shocked, ashamed, and speechless. He immediately left the hospital, wiping the spit off his face, with his head down, without looking Tom in the eye.

It was about the middle of the flight, and Sonjot was in the back of the plane.

The same little boy pretended to start shooting her and said, "I'm going to get you!"

Sonjot was looking on and felt disturbed by the little boy's behaviour. She rolled her eyes, exasperated, but his mother grabbed the little boy, told him to stay up front, to not go to the back, and to keep sitting in his seat.

A big storm with thunder and lightning caused turbulence, and the plane shook for a long time. The air traffic control personnel told the pilot to divert back to the Toronto airport because flying was too dangerous and asked the pilot to reschedule the flight for the next day.

When they announced this, Sonjot started yelling and screaming at the cabin crew. As the plane returned to Toronto, the little boy with the turban kept playfully shooting at Sonjot with his fingers from the front of the plane. As the flight descended in Toronto, she started to get anxious and paranoid. She told the flight attendant that she needed to board a plane for India as soon as possible, even if it meant making a layover in some other country and asked whether they were going to put them up at a hotel because she didn't want to go home. They said they would accommodate her wish, and her luggage would be sent to her room.

After leaving the airplane, she called Raj and told him what had happened. He told her not to panic and to tell the Singhs that she had to go see her ill mother and was stressed.

Raj said, "Their son is a drug addict, remember, and got into a big fight with his father. The father is on the other side of the country, so don't worry, my love. Remember, you're the beloved daughter-in-law. Hahaha!"

She said, "Okay, honey. Wow, you are smart!"

Raj told her to stay cool, calm, and collected.

Sonjot trusted Raj and believed the Singhs would believe her. So, she settled into her hotel room. She would be on her way to India by the next night. Early the next day, Crystal landed at the Toronto airport. Mr. Singh had given her a key to their house, but she went straight to the hospital to see Manjot and Manny. On seeing Manjot with an IV, she held her hand. Manjot, pleasantly surprised, looked at Crystal. She was wearing a turban with a Punjabi suit and a *kara*. They prayed together. Manjot told Crystal that she felt fine and was going to be released in a few hours. She also told her that she had been deliberately drugged but was going to be okay and asked her to help Manny and support him.

She said, "Yes, I will! I really love him. Where is he?"

She walked into Manny's room, and all the feelings of love and joy came back to Crystal. She saw that Manny didn't have a turban on.

She grabbed his hand and whispered, "You are my shining star, day and night! Love you for life, my love!" and started talking to him and praying.

She was by his side for a couple of hours. While unconscious, Manny was dreaming that Crystal was with him. He felt so peaceful and loved. They were at their secret spot, on top of the mountain, talking, holding hands, hugging, and kissing. Manny moved his hand while Crystal was holding it and praying. She couldn't believe it! Manny was dreaming about Crystal and saw her in his dreams and kept saying her name. She was so excited. She told Manjot over the phone because Manjot had gone home to change her clothes and was going to call the hospital in B.C. to see how her husband was doing. The doctors discovered from blood tests that all of them had drugs in their system. They said that someone had intentionally put drugs in their food or drinks. Manjot put two and two together and realized Sonjot was up to no good. She was recovering from the incident when she received a call from the bank manager informing her that her daughter-in-law had withdrawn $30,000. The bank manager had suspicions as to why she was acting nervously and withdrawing so much money. The bank manager had called their home but there was no answer at first. He tried numerous times to get hold of Mr. Singh and Manjot but couldn't succeed.

After Manjot discovered all the evil things Sonjot did, she called the police immediately and gave them all the information on Sonjot. The police tried to track her down to question her and possibly charge her with criminal offences.

Back at the hospital where Crystal was holding Manny's hands, she started to cry and kept calling his name, "Manny, Manny, Manny." He was now in and out of consciousness. Then, Crystal took off the *kara* that Manny had given her, put it on his wrist, and whispered, *"You have the heart of a lion. Roar, roar, my son! Life is gonna throw you off your bike, but you have to get on and start riding again, with or without pain."*

Manny, hearing the soft voice of his beloved and smelling her perfume, regained consciousness. He was still dazed but saying her name. She was so happy, she hugged and kissed him. The love of Manny's life was back. His shining star was on his side; his soul was complete again. He stood up stronger than ever and hugged his soulmate.

He prayed to the Guru and said, *"Waheguru, Waheguru!"*

He felt the *kara* and its love when she was holding his hand and praying to the power of the spiritual truth. Some tests still needed to be done, but the great news was Manny had emerged from his coma!

Hearing this good news about her little boy, Manjot rushed back to the hospital. She gave her boy the biggest hug and kiss. Tears of joy were rolling down her cheeks. She thanked Crystal for coming and staying with Manny. She praised her and told her that if not for her, Manny would not have come out of the coma. Crystal gave Manjot a big hug and told her she never had to say anything and that she loved Manny and would do anything for him. She also said that she greatly respected Manjot and Mr. Singh. Manjot said she had to leave to do something very important.

At the hospital in B.C., Tom would bring food and tea for Mr. Singh. He appreciated it and thanked Tom. Differences in skin colour and looks didn't matter to Mr. Singh anymore because it was a white fellow who was helping him, and all the white nurses were very nice to Mr. Singh and took good care of him. At the same time, his own brown friend, Jarnal, only visited him once for five minutes.

Mr. Singh heard the good news that his son was out of the coma and started to cry. Then he heard the bad news from his wife of what Sonjot had done. Manjot told him how Sonjot had taken $30,000 out of his bank account and drugged them all. He was fuming and apologized to Manjot for not believing her. He told Manjot to "find that *kooti* and slap her" for him.

Manjot had discovered that Sonjot had a flight booked to India that had gotten delayed to the next day.

Later that evening, Sonjot called the airline because she was supposed to board in a couple of hours, and her luggage never came. It had been accidentally sent to the family who was sitting right beside her, and someone would retrieve it from their hotel room. Sonjot couldn't wait, and when she went to find out where their room was, she couldn't believe it. She saw Manjot glaring at her with the eyes of a tiger about to catch its prey. Sonjot remembered to stay calm and relaxed as Raj had told her.

Then she went up to Manjot, somewhat nervously, and said, "Hi, mom! How's Manny? How's Dad? I had to take an emergency flight because my mother is sick."

Manjot didn't say a word and was looking straight into Sonjot's eyes like a cobra about to strike. Then it came, a big slap to Sonjot's face.

Manjot shouted, "How could you do this? You tricked our whole family into Manny getting married to you, and your goals were to be dishonest and against the Sikh religion. You bitch! You will get what is coming to you, I promise."

Sonjot fell to the ground with her hands grabbing on to Manjot's feet as if she wanted her to forgive her. Manjot didn't say a word. She saw and took out Manny's Rolex watch from Sonjot's purse.

Manjot said, "This is my precious boy's watch. It belongs to him. How can you be so evil and dishonest?"

Manjot had tracked down the luggage that was accidentally sent to the hotel room where the lady and young boy in the turban were staying. They found the phone number on the luggage and called Manjot's house, and she immediately called the police. As soon as Manjot had approached the room, the little boy had given her the watch. He looked like Manny when he was young. The little boy told Manjot that the watch had fallen out of Sonjot's seat while she was making a scene, which they told her all about. The police arrested Sonjot, and as for Raj, the Punjab Police arrested him in India.

CHAPTER 23

Mr. Singh fully recovered from the accident. The Singhs were very hurt by what Jarnal had done and decided to never talk to him again. Mr. Singh was disappointed in Jarnal, and he kept wondering why he did what he had done, especially when he had taken care of him in India, and they had lived side by side like brothers throughout childhood. Mr. Singh had sworn at Jarnal and punched him hard in the face for his wrongdoing. Jarnal fell to the ground, holding his eye. He said he was very sorry and didn't want to hurt his friend and confessed he was simply being greedy and selfish. Mr. Singh left, calling him a traitor. It was discovered from the gossiping relatives of Jarnal that he received a large sum of money for Manny's wedding, and the only reason he wanted Manny to get married was because of the money.

Manjot was even more unimpressed by Jarnal because of what he had done to her and her family and because he had tried to swindle many other families who came from India. Jarnal was never to be trusted by anyone in the community again, and everyone knew what type of man he was.

Kuljit confronted Karm on the phone from the mainland and told her everything about Jarnal. But being a typical Indian wife, Karm merely kept quiet. She thought to herself that Jarnal was a "piece of shit," but according to the Indian tradition, she had to stay with him and was helpless to leave.

Manjot told Mr. Singh her secret about what Jarnal had done to her. She said that she felt very ashamed and blamed herself, even if it was not her fault, and that her husband wouldn't understand. But she was relieved to tell the truth and to let go of her pain. Jarnal was no longer going to be in their lives anymore in any case. It was good that her husband had now seen Jarnal's true colours and was no longer under his spell.

Mr. Singh gave Manjot a big hug and held her in his arms. Tears ran down his cheeks. Manjot hadn't had a hug in a while. Instead of her husband blaming her, as usual, he was trying to show her affection because she had been through a lot and put up with a lot. Mr. Singh knew she didn't deserve how he had treated her. He wanted to show her that she was the real hero of the family for raising their son well. Manjot had tears in her eyes. Finally, Mr. Singh was being the man he was supposed to be, loving and caring.

He apologized to Manny and told him he was blindsided by everything that had happened with Sonjot, but all he ever wanted was the best for his son. Manny hugged his father and forgave him.

The Singhs eventually sold their house in Toronto and moved back to the mainland near Vancouver. Manjot was close by her *saheli*, Kuljit, again.

They gave Manny and Crystal the house up north. They got married and had two beautiful children.

Manny never wore a turban after his hair got cut. Mr. Singh didn't judge his son's decision; it was his choice, especially since Manny was very happily married to Crystal.

Mr. Singh had a new attitude towards Caucasian people and all different races and minorities. He realized that we are all the same—we bleed the same, and nobody is superior or inferior to the next person. Tom became his best friend. Dorothy and Manjot became great friends too, as well as now being family by marriage.

Mr. Singh went on to make many friends of all races, now that his narrow-minded way of thinking had ended. He found himself missing John and Bertha and appreciating how they helped raise their boy and did so much for their family. He would regularly contact their daughters and annually put money in a charity that John had loved. It was to help children who couldn't get the help they needed. John's daughters appreciated Mr. Singh for recognizing and respecting their late mother Bertha and their late father John, and he realized how lucky he was to be in a great country with nice people who cared for him and his family.

It took Mr. Singh a while to finally understand that the code embedded in him since birth to follow the faith and traditional ways had to change in the years to come. He was resigned to allowing fate to direct him and make him realize that one can't stand in the way of what's meant to be.

Mr. Singh adored his two lovely grandchildren, even though they were half white and half brown. He would visit, bringing them toys, candy, and clothes and giving them hugs and smiles every time they visited. He was very affectionate towards them and talked to his friends about them all the time.

Mr. Singh was a new man who had to go through a life-changing experience to see what mattered in life, which is happiness. He also discovered that everything was not always black and white. It didn't matter what religion or colour you were. In the end, we are all human, and that's what matters the most.

ABOUT THE AUTHOR

I, Satpal Sidhu, the Author of *Broken Turban*, go by the name Paul Sidhu. I'm from the Fraser Valley in British Columbia, east of Vancouver. I have lived here almost all my life and have two younger brothers and a son and a daughter. This book is dedicated to my second cousin, who was older than I was. He was my role model—I wanted to comb my hair as he did and wear the same kind of jacket he did. He paved the way for us; he broke the ice. He was one of the first Indian men to ever date someone outside of our culture, and it was big news back then. Everyone would gossip about him, and when I experienced a similar situation, I had to write about his story because what happened was very extreme. I started gathering information to write his story several years ago, and finally, I was able to put it together in 2021. Unfortunately, my second cousin and his parents passed on by the time I could give a shape to this book. This book is a look behind the scenes of never-talked-about real-life stories from first generation migrant Punjabi families—the hardships and struggles they experienced while in the process of settling in a new, foreign land, accepting and embracing a multicultural society, and imagining the life of the future generations.

GLOSSARY

- *aloo gobi*: potato and cauliflower mixture cooked with Indian spices
- *bada phea*: older brother
- *beta*: son
- *beti*: daughter
- *bhangra*: traditional Punjabi dance
- bindi: a mark, such as a red dot or piece of jewellery, worn on the middle of the forehead
- *bouddha*: old man
- *Buba*: Indian priest
- Christianity: an Abrahamic, monotheistic religion based on the life and teachings of Jesus of Nazareth. It is the world's largest religion.
- *chunni*: a piece of Indian clothing similar to a scarf
- Diwali: a festival of lights that is celebrated by many Hindu and Sikh families. It is particularly associated with Lakshmi, the goddess of prosperity, and marks the beginning of the fiscal year in India.

- *ek onkar*: one God
- *gora*: white male
- *goree*: white female
- Gurkhas: units in the British Army known for their khukuri (a distinctive heavy knife with a curved blade). They have a reputation for being fierce and brave soldiers.
- *Gurudwara*: "Door to the guru" is a place of assembly and worship for the Sikhs. People from all faiths are welcomed in *Gurudwaras*.
- *haldi*: turmeric
- Hindu: a person who practises Hinduism
- Hinduism: an Indian religion and dharma, or way of life. It is the world's third-largest religion with over 1.2 billion followers.
- Islam: an Abrahamic monotheistic religion, which teaches that Muhammed is a messenger of God. It is the world's second largest religion with 1.9 billion followers, known as Muslims, or 25% of the world's population.
- *kachchha*: cotton underwear
- *kamla*: stupid male
- *kamli*: stupid female
- *kangha*: wooden comb
- *kara*: steel bracelet
- *kesh*: uncut hair
- *kirpa*: mercy, grace, compassion, kindness
- *kirpan*: steel sword
- *kooti*: bitch

- *kota*: asshole
- *langar*: free food for everyone, regardless of their religion or background, served at the Sikh temple
- *lassi*: a combination of buttermilk and water
- *mahenga*: expensive
- *Maiyaan*: an Indian celebration the night before a wedding. It is a festival event in which the groom's female relatives put turmeric paste on him, dance, and sing songs of giving away the bride and groom.
- *manja*: bed about two feet high and four feet long made out of nylon webbing
- Muslim: a follower of Islam
- *paagal*: crazy
- Paki: derogatory term for a person from Pakistan
- *panchod*: sister fucker
- *pan-chottii*: slut, hooker
- *puth*: sweet kid
- roti: Indian flatbread
- *saheli*: a female friend
- samosa: a savoury snack made of flour with a filling of potatoes and peas
- sari: Indian suit for females
- *Sat Shri Akaal*: a form of Sikh greeting
- Sikhism: Religion that originated in the Punjab region of the Indian subcontinent around the end of the 15th century CE. It's the fifth-largest religion in the world.

- *Sant Sipahi*: Saint Soldier
- *subjee*: mixed Indian vegetables and spices
- *Waheguru*: almighty god, supreme soul, the creator in Sikhism, wonderous guru teacher
- *yar*: male friend

With every donation, a voice will be given to
the creativity that lies within the hearts of
our children living with diverse challenges.

By making this difference, children that may
not have been given the opportunity to have their
Heart Heard will have the freedom to create
beautiful works of art and musical creations.

Donate by visiting
HeartstobeHeard.com

We thank you.